The Creativity Tools Memory Jogger™

A Pocket Guide
for Creative Thinking

Diane Ritter & Michael Brassard

First Edition
GOAL/QPC

The Creativity Tools Memory Jogger™
A Pocket Guide for Creative Thinking

Development Team

Bob Page, *Project Sponsor*
Diane Ritter, *Project Leader and Co-author*
Michael Brassard, *Co-author*
Fran Oddo, *Editor and Author of Chapter 5*
Michele Kierstead, *Graphic Design and Layout*
Lori Champney, *Cover Design*
Steve Boudreau, *Graphics Production/Printing*
Carolyn Field, *Graphics Production*
Dorie Overhoff, *Marketing/Reader's Panel*
Paul Brassard, *Sales*
Bob King, *Advisor*
Richard Morrison, *Advisor*

GOAL/QPC

2 Manor Parkway, Salem, NH 03079-2841
Toll free: 1-800-643-4316 **or** 603-890-8800
Fax: 603-870-9122
E-mail: service@goalqpc.com
Web site: http://www.goalqpc.com

Printed in the United States of America

First Edition
10 9 8 7 6 5 4 3

ISBN 1-57681-021-6

Acknowledgments

Our thanks to the following people for their *creative* insights, suggestions, and encouragement throughout the development of this book.

Concept and Content Reviewers

Jill Snell, *Glaxo Wellcome Australia Ltd.*

Ted Cahill, *Phoenix Home Life*

Sarah Parsons, *Wyeth Ledard Vaccines and Pediatrics*

Patrick Cole, *Donnelly Corporation*

Stella Spalt, *Training 2000*

David Griffith, *Ford Motor Company*

Robert Forrest, *Puget Sound Naval Shipyard*

Laur Wasserbauer, *Federal Reserve Bank of Cleveland*

Dave Jones, *Caterpillar, Inc.*

Dorcas Hirzel, *Pullman Memorial Hospital*

Tracy Schmidt, *Tennessee Valley Authority*

Special thanks to:

Bob King, *GOAL/QPC*, for his vision in pursuing the research and development of the Creativity Tools.

Helmut Schlicksupp, *Innovationsbertung*, for his wisdom, patience, and understanding as our teacher of creativity.

Janice Marconi, *MarconiWorks*, for her initial research and development of the Creativity Tools course material and for providing the word lists for the Word Associations and Analogies tool.

Photo Credits

Marching band, Methuen (MA) High School "Rangers" Marching Band

Lighthouse and Geese, Diane Ritter

Cactus, Fran Oddo

How to Use
The Creativity Tools Memory Jogger™

The Creativity Tools Memory Jogger™ is designed for you to use as a convenient and quick reference guide on the job. Put your finger on any creativity tool within seconds!

Know the tool you need?

Find it by using the table of contents or the tool name printed at the bottom of each page.

Not sure what tool you need?

Get an idea by using the Tool Selector Guide on page *vii*. It organizes the tools into four key areas: restating the problem, generating ideas, transferring knowledge from other fields, and identifying combinations.

What do the different figures mean?

🏃 Getting Ready—An important first step is to select the right tool for the situation. When you see the "getting ready" position of the runner, expect a brief description of the tool's purpose and a list of benefits in using the tool.

🏃 Cruising—When you see this runner, expect to find construction guidelines. This is the action phase that provides you with step-by-step instructions.

🏃 Finishing the Course—When you see this runner, you are on the first page of the case example of a tool. These case examples, representing a variety of situations, highlight how a group or individuals applied the tool and where it lead them.

✅ Training Tips—When you see this figure, you'll get tips on tool use or team behavior.

Contents

Tool Selector Guide

	If you want to:	Then try:	Page
Restate the Problem	Articulate the problem/goal differently so that you can think about it differently	• Knowledge Mapping • Problem Reformulation • Purpose Hierarchy	• 55 • 97 • 119
Generate Ideas	Get people to think up a lot of ideas	• Brainwriting 6-3-5 • Classic Brainstorming	• 21 • 31
Transfer Knowledge	Draw on ideas, facts, and/or principles from other fields of knowledge	• Imaginary Brainstorming • Picture Associations & Biotechniques • TILMAG • Word Associations & Analogies	• 39 • 83 • 133 • 147
Identify Combinations	Expand your view of all the possible solutions to your problem or goal	• Morphological Box	• 71

The Creativity Tools complement improvement techniques such as the Basic QC Tools and the Management and Planning Tools. These planning and improvement tools (featured in *The Memory Jogger™ II*) have been invaluable in finding root causes and developing plans that work. People around the world have made valuable contributions and improvements in their organizations, and now with the Creativity Tools, they will be better equipped to find breakthroughs in their organization's processes, products, and services.

Thanks to:

For:

Our sources of
inspiration, creativity, love
and support.

Chapter **1**

Why Do We Need Creativity?

It is crucial for today's organizations . . .

The field of organizational excellence has evolved significantly over the last 20 years. Continuous improvement is still at the heart of any organizational excellence process, but it alone isn't enough to ensure that organizations will survive and thrive in today's VERY competitive marketplace.

Innovative organizations are working to combine this incremental approach to improvement with "revolutionary ideas" that will help them surpass their competition. Organizations need people at all levels that can help achieve this balanced approach to problems and market opportunities.

The Old Approach to Creativity

- Only a few people in any organization were considered "the creative ones."
- Breakthrough ideas are needed only in the "strategic" areas of the business.
- Engineers were routinely brought in to fix major production or customer problems.
- Consultants were hired to help achieve a breakthrough in products and markets.

Why doesn't this approach work today? Most companies and markets are experiencing major changes on a monthly, weekly, and in some cases, daily basis. The old approach to creativity can't produce dramatic results fast enough.

The New Approach to Creativity

- Breakthroughs are required in every corner of a competitive organization.
- Specialists in breakthroughs (e.g., engineers, consultants) are still critical, but more people must become involved in creatively tackling the increasing number of challenges that are emerging.
- The creativity that exists naturally within everyone in the organization must be harnessed.
- A common process for dramatic improvement must be created.

What it means to be creative . . .

Being creative involves:

- Consistently producing a lot of ideas.
- Putting existing or new ideas together in different combinations.
- Breaking an idea down to take a fresh look at its parts.
- Making connections between the topic at hand and seemingly unrelated facts, events or observations.

The purpose of the Creativity Tools . . .

Innovative organizations have come to realize that every person needs to contribute his or her experience and creativity. However, some people have more fully developed their ability to piece ideas together creatively and to communicate them clearly.

Some blame traditional forms of education for rewarding rational thinking and solutions over creative approaches. Others place more emphasis on "natural" creativity. All agree that much more can be done to bring out our natural creativity. This is the purpose of the Creativity Tools.

How to use the Creativity Tools

The Creativity Tools provide a structured way for an individual, group, or team to combine intuition, imagination, and personal experience to create interesting, and eventually, innovative concepts and solutions. These innovative solutions can be aimed at virtually any target:

- reducing cost and waste
- developing new products and services
- resolving long-standing customer complaints
- dramatically cutting down cycle time
- developing new processes or dramatic process improvements

The Creativity Tools also enhance the creativity process by:

- breaking people's routine patterns of thinking
- consistently inspiring breakthrough ideas
- enhancing traditional brainstorming methods
- surfacing the creative potential of all employees
- turbo-charging continuous improvement activities

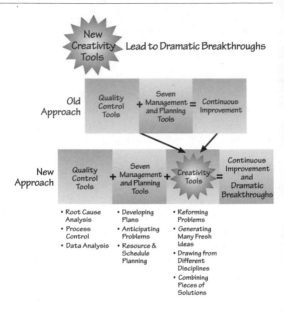

New Creativity Tools Lead to Dramatic Breakthroughs

Old Approach

Quality Control Tools + Seven Management and Planning Tools = Continuous Improvement

New Approach

Quality Control Tools + Seven Management and Planning Tools + Creativity Tools = Continuous Improvement and Dramatic Breakthroughs

- Root Cause Analysis
- Process Control
- Data Analysis

- Developing Plans
- Anticipating Problems
- Resource & Schedule Planning

- Reforming Problems
- Generating Many Fresh Ideas
- Drawing from Different Disciplines
- Combining Pieces of Solutions

The most important thing to remember is that the Creativity Tools work best when an organization is interested in achieving dramatic improvements with widespread participation.

Chapter *2*

Setting the Stage for the Creativity Tools

What environment draws out natural creativity?

The Creativity Tools are proving to be very helpful to organizations in North America and Europe in drawing out the natural creativity that lies within individuals and teams.

The organizations that are reaping the most rewards from the Creativity Tools are also those with environments that encourage creative thinking.

Perhaps lessons can be learned from environments that are synonymous with natural creativity. What do a research and development lab, a children's playground, or a musician's studio all have in common? They are all environments that encourage people to explore and experiment with ideas and behaviors.

How can organizations help to develop this type of environment along with the creativity that flows from it?

In a creative environment . . .

- *There is freedom from criticism* . . . people can experiment and take risks without embarrassment.
- *Making connections and building upon ideas are encouraged* . . . ideas are constantly shared so that each person can see unusual and powerful new combinations, like children inventing a new game to play.

- *All ideas are recognized and acknowledged* . . . a two-way flow of communication is essential. Ideas must have a place to go and once they get there, people should know if they'll be used, discussed further or rejected, and why.
- *There is respect for different gifts* . . . the different ways that people express their intelligence and talents must be seen as an asset, not as a liability to be overcome.
- *The outside world is a place to be explored, not feared* . . . information about the broader world must be made visible and available. Experience the world as your customer does. It clarifies both your purpose and the nature of your challenge.
- *Playfulness is encouraged* . . . humor is encouraged as a way to keep perspective on issues. Seeing the lighter side of an issue often provides just the distance that's needed to take a fresh approach.

> "There's a world of difference between being somber and being serious."
>
> *John Cleese, British humorist*

What behaviors encourage creativity?

The most powerful tool for creativity is personal behavior. What can all individuals do to bring out their own creativity and that of the people around them?

To be a catalyst for creativity you must . . .

- *Respect yourself and others* . . . acknowledge your own skills and experience, AND your limitations. Asking for someone's help is a fundamental sign of respect.

- *Actively listen* . . . always confirm your understanding of a person's idea. This will ensure that the idea is more clearly understood by listener and speaker alike, and the person who's speaking can further develop the idea throughout the interaction.

- *Believe that everyone is fallible (especially yourself)* . . . enough said!

- *Interact, interact, interact* . . . get out of your office, pose questions, listen to the responses, pose questions, stimulate debate . . . when you don't know quite what to do, find people to think with you. The problem often gets deeper when you think about it in isolation.

- *Avoid "killer phrases[1] "* . . . replace "We've done that before . . ." with "Can you tell me more . . ."; replace "Our customers would never buy that!" with "Say more about how it would help our customers." Your job is to help people bring their ideas to life. Killer phrases stop ideas dead in their tracks.

- *Assume that "the cement is always wet" until an idea has to be finalized for implementation* . . . present potential solutions with rough edges that can be smoothed with the help of others. Even when the concept is fully developed, ALWAYS present it as an open question. You may be surprised by the questions you've missed.

- *Be an explorer* . . . read, surf the internet, visit customers, enjoy the arts, watch children play . . . do ANYTHING to prevent yourself from becoming a prisoner of your own knowledge, experience, and current view of the world.

---

[1]Charles "Chic" Thompson, *What a Great Idea: The Key Steps Creative People Take* (New York: HarperPerennial, 1992), 23.

What is the relationship between creativity and innovation[2]?

Creativity, at its most basic level, is the process of generating many ideas. *Innovation* is the process of selecting/combining, refining, and turning the best creative idea(s) into reality. Both are EQUALLY important for organizations to be competitive.

Today's organizations are operating with very little margin for error, and few can afford to generate endless ideas that never see the light of the marketplace.

One of the major challenges is to *efficiently* generate as many creative ideas as possible (the Creativity Tools) and then *efficiently* convert them into products and services (the Management & Planning Tools). When these tool sets are combined with the appropriate environment and behaviors, an organization can generate both product breakthroughs and a workplace that stimulates every person to be creative.

---

[2]For a more complete discussion on the relationship between creativity and innovation, see *The Idea Edge*, pp. ix–xiv, by Bob King and Helmut Schlicksupp (GOAL/QPC, 1998).

Chapter **3**

Putting the Creativity Tools into an Organizational Improvement Context

Structured approaches to process improvement and problem solving focus primarily (and rightfully so) on the identification of root causes. Most of these processes, however, assume that good ideas and solutions will naturally flow once the root causes have been identified.

This does often happen . . . but what happens when tried (and tired) solutions are the only ideas being proposed? How can a situation or problem be redefined to create an entirely fresh approach?

This is the strength of integrating the Creativity Tools with other tool sets such as the Basic Quality Control (QC) Tools and the Management & Planning (MP) Tools. (The QC and MP Tools are described in *The Memory Jogger™ II*.)

The context for using these tools is a process-improvement and problem-solving model with a standard set of steps and actions, such as the model described in the following section. This seven-step improvement model is generic enough to apply to any situation and allows you to use any combination of tools to help you collect data, document a process, find root causes, generate and select new ideas for a new solution, and successfully implement your organization's creative ideas.

Use the matrix on pages 12–13 to see how the Creativity Tools, the QC Tools, and the MP Tools are best integrated within the seven-step improvement model.

The Seven-Step Improvement Model¹

| Plan |

1. **Select the problem/process that will be addressed first (or next) and describe the improvement opportunity.**
   - Ask "What's wrong?" and "What's not working?"
   - Look for changes in important business indicators.
   - Assemble and support the right team.
   - Collect and review customer data, define customer's problem or opportunity.
   - Narrow down project focus.
   - Develop project purpose statement.

2. **Describe the current process surrounding the improvement opportunity.**
   - Map out and describe the current process.
   - Validate map with current process users.
   - Collect data.
   - Select the relevant process or segment to further refine the scope of the project.

3. **Describe all of the possible causes of the problem and agree on the root cause(s).**
   - Ask "Why?" five times.

---

¹This model is also described on pp. 115–131 in *The Memory Jogger™ II*.

- Identify cause(s) of the problem.
- Verify root cause(s) with data whenever possible.

4. **Develop an effective and workable solution and action plan, including targets for improvement.**
   - Generate potential solutions.
   - Define, rank, and analyze solutions.
   - Select solution that best meets customer needs.
   - Plan the change process.
   - Do contingency planning when dealing with new and risky plans.
   - Determine resources.
   - Set targets for improvement and establish monitoring methods.

5. **Implement the solution or process change.**
   - Implement.
   - Collect more data for subsequent assessment.
   - Follow the plan and monitor the milestones and measures.

Steps continued on page 14

Use this matrix to identify which tools are best used within each of the seven steps of the improvement model. The matrix also identifies which tools are best

Adding the Creativity Tools to a Seven-Step Improvement Model

Key:
○ Fact Finding
● Idea Generation
△ Idea Selection
□ Idea Implementation

Steps	Activity Network Diagram	Affinity Diagram	Brainwriting 6-3-5	Cause & Effect Diagram	Classic Brainstorming	Control Chart	Flowchart	Gantt Chart	Histogram	Imaginary Brainstorming	Interrelationship Digraph
1. Select the problem/process		● △			●	○			○		
2. Describe current process							○ ●				
3. Describe causes			●	○	●	○			○	●	△
4. Develop solution(s)	□	●			●			□			
5. Implement solution(s)	□					○		□	○		
6. Review/evaluate result(s)						○	□		○		
7. Reflect/act on learnings		●	●		●						

used for fact finding, idea generation, idea selection, or idea implementation.

Adding the Creativity Tools to a Seven-Step Improvement Model

Steps	Knowledge Mapping	Matrix Diagram	Morphological Box	Nominal Group Technique	Pareto Chart	Picture Assoc./Biotechniques	Prioritization Matrices	Problem Reformulation	Process Decision Program Ch.	Purpose Hierarchy	Radar Chart	Run Chart	Scatter Diagram	TILMAG	Tree Diagram	Word Associations/Analogies
1.	●△				○		△	●△		●△		○				
?								●								
3.	●		●	△	○	●						○	○	●		●
4.		△□		△			△□								□	
5.		□						□	□			○			□	
6.				○								○	○			
7.		□							□	△					□	

6. Review and evaluate the result of the change.
  - Review the results of the change. Is the solution having the desired effect? Any unintended consequences?
  - Revise the process, as necessary.
  - Standardize the improvement to hold the gain.
  - Establish measures for monitoring the process for changes.

Act

7. Reflect and act on learnings.
  - Assess the results and problem-solving processes; recommend changes.
  - Continue the improvement process where needed; standardize where possible.
  - Seek other opportunities for improvement.
  - Evaluate lessons the team learned from the experience; what can be improved?
  - Celebrate success.

Integrating the Creativity Tools with Major Creativity Approaches

People have been thinking about and discussing the nature of creativity for centuries. However, since the early 1950s there has been an incredible rise in the number of people studying and writing about this subject.

There are three people whose work has become particularly well known in the business world: Alex Osborn, George Prince, and Edward de Bono.

Alex Osborn introduced, among other things, the concept of brainstorming and its widely known guidelines in his classic book, *Applied Imagination* (1953).

Then in 1960, George Prince developed the creative problem-solving method known as synectics. It is used by teams to solve tough problems by discovering links between ideas and things that appear at first glance to be disconnected.

Edward de Bono, in *The Mechanism of Mind* (1969), introduced a third major concept in creativity, known as lateral thinking. It involves trying different perceptions, concepts, and points of entry to come at a problem from many different angles. De Bono refers to this as "thinking sideways about a problem."

Alex Osborn

In addition to his contributions in the area of brainstorming, Osborn is also associated with creating checklists of questions that stimulate creativity. Bob Eberle added other questions to form the well-known SCAMPER acronym.[2]

---

[2]Michael Michalko, *Thinkertoys: A Handbook of Business Creativity for the 90s* (Berkeley, CA: Ten Speed Press, 1991), 73.

- What can be **S**ubstituted for …?
- What can be **C**ombined with … ?
- How can … be **A**dapted?
- How can … be **M**odified or **M**inified?
- How can … be **P**ut to other uses?
- How can … be **E**liminated?
- What if … were **R**eversed or **R**earranged?

These are intriguing questions that can be made even more interesting by using the Creativity Tools to provide a little structure and a lot of room for imagination. How do these tools add value to SCAMPER? See table below.

Creativity Tools	Value to SCAMPER
• Classic Brainstorming	• Simple and familiar listing of ideas can be used to answer any SCAMPER question.
• Imaginary Brainstorming • Picture Associations and Biotechniques • Word Associations and Analogies	• Team Members: – "Leave the problem" – Use their imagination – Apply the ideas to the "real" problem. Makes it easier for team members to "stretch" their answers to most of the SCAMPER questions.
• Knowledge/Mind Mapping	• Teams/Individuals: – Use a simple visual method to unleash a stream of connected ideas. Ideal for creating the free flow of ideas that the SCAMPER questions generate.

George Prince

Synectics is based on the Greek word, "synektiktein" meaning "bringing forth together" or "bringing different things into unified connection." As a creativity technique, it uses metaphors and analogies to help teams achieve breakthroughs. It also tries to combine ideas that appear to be opposites.

Among the Creativity Tools featured in this book, **Classic Brainstorming** provides the most direct support to the synectics process. The well-known guidelines of this technique form the foundation for the synectics process. **Imaginary Brainstorming, Picture Associations/Biotechniques, Word Associations and Analogies**, and **TILMAG** are powerful complements to synectics. Each tool provides a structured way to make unusual connections and associations.

Edward de Bono

Edward de Bono starts from the same set of assumptions that underlie the Creativity Tools. First, creativity is not about being crazy or unconventional. Creativity occurs when we take advantage of the self-organizing patterns that occur in all thinking.[3]

Secondly, creativity can be encouraged and accelerated by simple techniques such as provocation or "po." Simply put, "po" is a statement that disrupts our normal flow of thinking so that we can form new ideas and concepts.

For example, "Running shoes should be heavy." This is certainly not the "normal" starting point for designing a new running shoe. However, just imagine the new lines of thinking that this "po" would start in motion.

---

[3]Edward de Bono, *Serious Creativity* (New York: HarperCollins, 1993), 4.

As in de Bono's work, all of the Creativity Tools are designed to uncover interesting patterns among ideas. In addition, almost all of them use a stimulating word, image or new context to encourage fresh ideas.

For example, **Problem Reformulation** visually shows the system surrounding a problem in order to show new approaches to old problems. **Imaginary Brainstorming** breaks old thought patterns by placing a problem in an imaginary new context. **Picture Associations/ Biotechniques, Word Associations and Analogies,** and **TILMAG** stimulate new connections by introducing images and words that temporarily derail traditional patterns of thought in order to explore interesting, new territory.

Finally, the **Morphological Box** allows a team to put ideas from any source (a "po" statement or one of the Creativity Tools) into interesting combinations.

Creative people and organizations will find ways to combine all of these approaches to generate innovative solutions. The question is not, "What's the BEST approach to creativity?" but rather, "What method or combination of methods will move our thinking to unexplored territory?"

Chapter 4

The Creativity Tools

Just as the tools for quality control (QC) and management and planning (MP) help people to visualize, organize, and analyze *data*, the Creativity Tools help people to visualize, organize, and analyze *new ideas* that lead to solving problems, developing new products, and improving processes.

The Creativity Tools

The listing below groups the Creativity Tools into four areas to help you better understand how the tools are related to each other and to the accomplishment of certain "tasks." Use the grouped list below if you know the "task" you'd like to accomplish but you don't know which tools are most appropriate for the task.

If you need to find a tool fast, use the table of contents at the front of the book or on the previous page to "instantly" find the page you need.

> Articulate the problem differently so you see it differently

Restating the Problem

> Think up a lot of ideas (the familiar, some new and some unusual)

Generating Ideas

Transferring Knowledge from Other Fields

> Borrow ideas, facts, principles from other fields

Identifying Combinations

> Expand your view of all the possible solutions to your problem

Brainwriting 6-3-5
Building on each other's ideas

Why use it?

To provide the time and structure for team members to thoughtfully generate a large number of ideas and to find unusual connections and combinations among those ideas.

What does it do?

- Provides a worksheet for team members to record their ideas.
- Combines the energy of exchanging ideas and the thoughtfulness of a nonverbal, written process.
- Defuses emotional issues that may reduce the participation and creative flow of ideas among team members.
- When compared to Classic Brainstorming, this tool more consistently builds synergy among team members' ideas.

How do I do it?

1. **Assemble the team and clarify the issue.**
   - The ideal number of team members is six but a smaller or larger group can also use this tool.
   - Clarify the topic of the session. Consider using one of the problem statements identified with Problem Reformulation, if this tool was previously used.

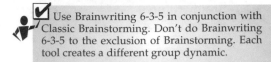

Use Brainwriting 6-3-5 in conjunction with Classic Brainstorming. Don't do Brainwriting 6-3-5 to the exclusion of Brainstorming. Each tool creates a different group dynamic.

2. **Complete the 6-3-5 worksheets.**
   - The name Brainwriting 6-3-5 comes from the process of having 6 people write 3 ideas within 5 minutes.
   - Each person has a blank 6-3-5 worksheet.

Sample Problem Statement:
"How can police officers establish positive relationships with kids in the community?"

	1	2	3
1			
2			
3			
4			
5			
6			

a) Each person records the problem statement at the top of the worksheet. Everyone should write the same problem statement, word for word.

b) Everyone writes three ideas in the top row of the worksheet within a five-minute time frame. Avoid talking during the writing process. Take the full five minutes to develop the ideas but also allow your ideas to flow freely, without editing them excessively.

- Write each idea as a concise but complete sentence; 6–10 words works well.
- *Neatly* write one idea per box so other team members can read the ideas.
- Sometimes it's difficult to think of three ideas. If so, just leave a box blank.

If you're stuck in developing an idea, try asking yourself questions like: "Do I have any experience related to this idea that I can draw upon?" "Does this idea make me think of a similar experience?" Or even, "If I were a little kid, what would I come up with?"

As an alternative to writing directly on the worksheet, write each idea on a 3" x 3" Post-it™ Note and place it within one of the boxes on a worksheet enlarged to 11" x 17" size. The notes can be removed later for sorting and grouping. (See the Affinity Diagram chapter in *The Memory Jogger™ II*, page 12.)

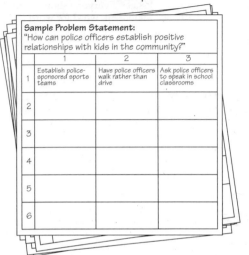

Example of Step 2b

Sample Problem Statement:
"How can police officers establish positive relationships with kids in the community?"

	1	2	3
1	Establish police-sponsored sports teams	Have police officers walk rather than drive	Ask police officers to speak in school classrooms
2			
3			
4			
5			
6			

c) At the end of five minutes—or when everyone is finished writing—pass the worksheet to the person on your right. If all of the members have completed the round in less than the five minutes provided, check to make sure everyone is finished, and then move to the next round.

d) Circulate the worksheets until they are completed.

- With each pass, read all the ideas written on the worksheet to stimulate your own thinking, and then generate three more ideas. Remember to:
  - Expand on an idea
  - Write a variation of any previous idea
  - Generate a completely unrelated new idea

If there are fewer than six people, circulate the worksheets until they are complete. For a team larger than six, provide additional worksheets or divide into subteams, then circulate the worksheets until they are complete.

When the group gets to rounds 5 and 6, participants may need more than 5 minutes per round to be able to read through all the previous ideas and to generate new ones.

3. **Analyze the ideas and select the best ones.**
   - Review all the ideas.
     - Eliminate any exact duplicates, but remember to keep any variations or extensions of ideas.
     - As a team, review the ideas for clarity.
   - If Post-it™ Notes were used, remove them for sorting and grouping. (See the Affinity Diagram chapter in *The Memory Jogger™ II*, page 12.)
   - Come to consensus around one to three ideas to pursue further. Use the Nominal Group Technique (*The Memory Jogger™ II*, page 91) or Prioritization Matrices (*The Memory Jogger™ II*, page 105) to narrow down the list of ideas that the team can work on.

Sample Problem Statement:
"How can police officers establish positive relationships with kids in the community?"

	1	2	3
1	Establish police-sponsored sports teams	Have police officers walk rather than drive	Ask police officers to speak in school classrooms
2	Let police officers teach a regular or weekly class	Establish police-sponsored events	Have a police-sponsored scout troop
3	Create trading cards featuring local police officers	Have kids adopt a cop	Organize rock concerts around a theme
4	Have officers live in the same neighborhoods as the kids	Have officers tutor kids on their homework	Have families invite police officers for dinner
5	Have police officers hold holiday parties	Have police officers raise money for scholarships for neighborhood kids	Ask police officers to volunteer to take in foster kids from the neighborhood
6	Give officers on-the-job psychology classes to better understand kids	Have a family help line staffed by officers	Organize a junior officer club

Variations

Brainwriting Pool

Each team member, using Post-it™ Notes or index cards, writes down ideas and places them in the center of the table. Everyone is free to pull one or more from this pool for inspiration. Team members can create new ideas, variations, or piggyback on ideas.

Using Post-it™ Notes is useful when a team wants to further develop the ideas with the Affinity Diagram or a similar tool.

Idea Card Method

Each team member, using Post-it™ Notes or index cards, writes down ideas and then piles them next to the person on his or her right. Each person draws from the "neighbor's" pile of ideas as needed. Once the idea is used, it is passed on to the next team member. Any new ideas generated from the "inspiration" idea are also passed on.

Collective Notebook Method

Another form of Brainwriting 6-3-5 uses notebooks for team members to collect their ideas as they come to mind, any time, any place. Each team member records in the notebook: a description of the problem, any specified requirements for a solution, and additional, relevant objectives. Team members record ideas, thoughts, and images over a period of time, typically two to four weeks. All notebooks are collected, consolidated, and discussed at future team meetings.

> ✔ The Notebook Method can easily be adapted for use on any computer network/intranet system. In fact, using this technology allows people to share information in real time. It makes it possible for team members to build on each other's ideas and detect patterns among their ideas as they are generated.

Case Example:
Main Street Bank & Trust

The Tale:

The board of directors of Main Street Bank
& Trust is looking for a breakthrough approach
to distinguish itself in a very competitive
mortgage market.

The Time:

The team met for one hour following a
"Banking on You" appreciation dinner.

The Task:

1. Assemble the team and clarify the issue.

The bank president, a vice president, a branch
manager, three local homeowners, and three
potential mortgage customers formed a team.

The team's mission was to generate creative
ideas on how to attract and keep residential
mortgage customers.

2. Complete the 6-3-5 worksheets.

Sample Problem Statement: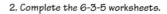
"How can we attract and keep residential mortgage customers?"

	1	2	3
1	Offer competitive rates	Offer help lines for first-time buyers	Develop an easy-to-follow road map through the mortgage process
2	Provide pre-qualification services	Provide free mortgage consultations	Go to a customer's home or workplace
3	Offer different mortgage programs for different income levels	Shorten the turn-around time for approving mortgage applications	Fill in the mortgage application for the customer
4	Provide mortgage information and resources on the bank's web site	Decentralize the mortgage approval authority to local branch managers	Offer mortgage applications in different languages
5	Put the mortgage application, with prompts, on the bank's web site	Focus on real service. Ben Franklin said: "Well done is better than well said."	Have multilingual mortgage loan officers
6	Work out a referral system with non-mortgage granting banks	Invite mortgage holders to an annual reunion picnic	Have automatic pro forma applications on the web site

3. Analyze the ideas and select the best ones.

The Tally:

The team's brainwriting effort surfaced many good individual ideas. It also allowed the team to step back and see patterns and make connections that, at first glance, no individual would have made alone. Every idea was documented, which made team members feel good about their effort to contribute ideas. In the end, the team decided to further explore the strategy of high-tech, state-of-the-art banking for its mortgage customers and combine it with good old-fashioned service.

Classic Brainstorming
*Creating bigger
& better ideas*

Why use it?

To get team members to pool their knowledge and creativity, in generating "waves" of ideas in a process that is free of criticism.

What does It do?

- Discourages "same old way" thinking by creating more and more ideas that team members can build upon.
- Gets all team members enthusiastic and involved by putting an equal value on every idea.
- Allows each person to be creative while focusing on a team's common purpose.
- Pulls out the known ideas within a team to allow new and creative ideas to emerge.

How do I do it?

1. **Identify the appropriate team to conduct the brainstorming session.**

   - Create a draft topic statement. Define the topic of the session to the point that an initial team can be identified and formed. Consider using the possible problem statements identified with Problem Reformulation, if this tool was previously used.

2. **Convene the team and clarify the topic and ground rules.**

   - Write the initial topic statement on a flipchart, whiteboard, or pinboard.

- Make sure that everyone understands the question, issue, or problem. Change or eliminate words that can be interpreted differently, and revise the topic statement.

- Review the ground rules of brainstorming:

  - Avoid criticizing ideas. Every idea is potentially a great one as long as it's clearly stated.

  - Quantity, quantity, quantity! Come up with as many ideas as possible as quickly as possible. Brainstorming sessions typically last 10 to 15 minutes. Clearly communicate the time limit.

  - Encourage a "free-wheeling" atmosphere. Don't censor your own ideas or anyone else's.

  - Listen to other team members' ideas and consciously find a connection that you can build upon. This is often referred to as "piggybacking" on ideas.

  - Avoid any discussion about the merits of ideas. Any discussions should focus on clarifying, not debating ideas.

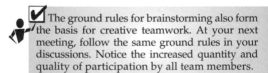

The ground rules for brainstorming also form the basis for creative teamwork. At your next meeting, follow the same ground rules in your discussions. Notice the increased quantity and quality of participation by all team members.

3. **Generate ideas.**

   - Select either the structured or unstructured method. Either method can be done silently or aloud.

Structured: As team members contribute ideas in turn, any member can pass at any time.

Unstructured: Team members give ideas as they come to mind. There is no need to "pass" since ideas are not solicited in rotation.

> ✅ With either method, it is always helpful to give people some quiet time to generate their own ideas before they participate as a team. Remember: "Some people think to talk, while others talk to think." Allowing this quiet time is a good way to balance participation by all.

- Recruit someone to record the ideas on a flipchart. Write each idea in large, visible letters. The person recording can also contribute ideas.

  – Record each idea in the same words of the speaker. Team members should ask for clarification, if necessary.

  – If an idea is very long, the speaker should condense it without losing its original meaning.

- Generate ideas through several cycles, or phases.

  – Keep the process moving and relatively short; 10 to 15 minutes works well.

  – At first ideas may come "rapid fire." These ideas are usually not new. With time, ideas become fewer and there are dead points, moments of silence, which mark the beginning of a new phase of brainstorming. As a team moves through these phases, fewer ideas come to mind, but these are often the most original.

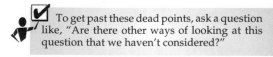

To get past these dead points, ask a question like, "Are there other ways of looking at this question that we haven't considered?"

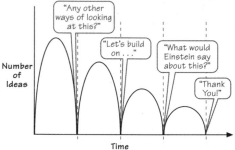

Four-phase Classic Brainstorming

"Any other ways of looking at this?"

"Let's build on . . ."

"What would Einstein say about this?"

"Thank You!"

Number of Ideas

Time

4. **Clarify ideas and conclude the brainstorming session.**

- Review the written list of ideas for clarity.
- Discard ideas only if they are virtually identical. It is often important to preserve subtle differences that are revealed in slightly different wordings.
- Come to consensus around a few ideas to discuss further and plan follow-up action.

Case Example:
Reducing the "Downtime" of Copy Machines

The Tale:

The operations manager of United Insurance realized that the lack of efficiency of copy machines throughout the company had become a major issue of concern.

The Time:

A one hour meeting.

The Task:

1. **Identify the appropriate team to conduct the brainstorming session.**

   The operations manager led a team consistenting of two department managers, a purchasing manager, and two administrative assistants.

2. **Convene the team and clarify the topic and ground rules.**

   Topic: To make copy machines an efficient part of the operation by maximizing their availablity to workers.

3. **Generate ideas.**

Phase One Ideas

- Train everyone how to operate the machines properly
- Buy better paper
- Train someone in preventive maintenance
- Contract with a repair company that has quick turn around
- Set a maximum number of copies that can be made

- Put a lock and key on it; limit access
- Keep the area free of dust
- Buy a machine only after a trial period
- Train people in emergency repair
- Have a back-up copier
- Don't rely on only one copier

> These last two ideas are similar but can lead to different outcomes. Keep them.

Phase Two Ideas
(Are there other ways of looking at this question that we haven't considered?)

- Buy from a manufacturer that uses SPC to make its machines
- Require all employees to clear up their own jams
- Designate a different machine for copying overhead transparencies—they tend to jam more often than paper

Phase Three Ideas
(Let's build on "Don't rely on only one copier.")

- Have an agreement to borrow/use a neighboring company's copier
- Have more than one copier on each floor
- Work with a supplier that gives you a "loaner"
- Have a lot of carbon paper on hand

> It seems silly, but you never know!

Phase Four Ideas
(What would the CEO say?)

- Negotiate a no-cost agreement with a copy center for instant service
- Ask, "Do I really need this copy?"
- Use e-mail
- Make reports available on an internal web site

> Sometimes the most interesting idea can be the last desperate try.

4. Clarify ideas and conclude the brainstorming session.

The Tally:
The team chose the three most promising ideas to discuss in more detail.

(1) "Do I really need this copy?"

The last idea spurred them to look at the copies being made. In their review of several standard reports, they agreed to eliminate two reports and to cut half the names from the distribution lists of three other reports.

(2) "Train someone in preventative maintenance."

They decided to train a staff person to do preventive maintenance on the copy machine rather than wait for a repair company to send someone over.

(3) "Have agreement to borrow/use a neighboring company's copier."

The team set up a mutual agreement with a few neighboring companies to use each other's copiers in emergency situations.

Imaginary Brainstorming
Brainstorming with a twist

Why use it?

To allow teams or individuals to break traditional patterns of thinking that can prevent creative solutions.

What does it do?

- Allows teams to come up with ideas that are radically different from other brainstorming sessions.
- Helps teams to separate themselves from the practical details of the problem that may be restricting their creative ideas.
- The imaginary aspect allows people to share "wild and crazy" ideas they may normally keep to themselves.
- It can bring energy and fun to even the most mundane issue.

How do I do it?

1. **Define the goal or problem.**
   - As in Classic Brainstorming, the problem statement should be clearly understood by all team members.
   - Pay special attention to the structure of the statement. Make sure it contains at least a subject (*who's acting*), verb (*the action*), and object (*who or what is being acted upon*). These will be the elements used in Step 3.

> ## Sample Problem Statement
>
> "How can we publish a book in half the time?"

2. **Generate and record ideas using Classic Brainstorming.**

> ### Brainstormed ideas for the real problem
> - Create a partnership with a printer
> - Outsource the cover design
> - Recruit a different author for each chapter
> - Partner with a design and publishing firm
> - Design cover internally
> - Assign someone to obtain copyright permissions throughout the project
> - Recruit reader panel members early!
> - Reward/penalize the team for keeping to the schedule
> - Identify the desired components from previous books
> - Borrow from other internal publications
> - Get customer input up front and throughout the project
> - Resolve all design issues up front
> - Prevent others from using committed desktop publishing resources

- No non-project-related commitments for authors
- Keep "it" internal
- Train/orient other editors early
- Assign proofreading to non-editors
- Examine alternate ways to produce reader panel versions
- More planning on graphics
- Sketch graphics before finalizing layout
- Create examples up front
- Decide on physical limitations of the book up front
- Develop and write to a template
- Get somebody to provide administrative support for all authors
- Conduct the internal review process earlier

3. **Define the essential elements of the problem or goal statement.**

- The subject, verb, and object of a sentence communicate the essence of any statement. These are the elements that may be changed in the second round of brainstorming.

- Ask the who, what, and where of the problem:

  – Who or what is performing an action?

  – Who or what is the recipient of the action?

  – What is the action being performed?

  – Where is the action being performed?

  – Are there any other elements directly involved in the dynamics of the problem?

Identify the one element that is most directly tied to a successful solution; feel free to change any other element except for this one.

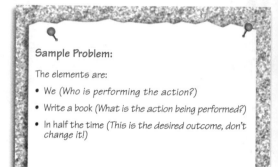

Sample Problem:

The elements are:

- We (*Who is performing the action?*)
- Write a book (*What is the action being performed?*)
- In half the time (*This is the desired outcome, don't change it!*)

4. **Propose imaginary replacements for one of the elements of the problem statement.**

- Make sure the imaginary replacements are radically different from the original element to break the team's fixed patterns of thinking.
- Have fun in generating imaginary replacements.

Sample Substitutions

	Effective	Ineffective
We	• Children • Koko the gorilla	• Men/women • Our department
Write a book	• Get a college degree • Build a house • Pay the bills • Retire	• Write a brochure • Develop software
In half the time	Essential characteristic of the solution, don't substitute here!	

5. **Formulate a new problem statement, substituting one of the imaginary elements.**

   • Change one, and only one, element at a time. This prevents a team from getting so far away from the original context of the problem that it cannot apply the creative ideas back to the real problem.

Sample Imaginary Problem Statement

"How do we <u>build</u> a house in half the time?"

6. **Brainstorm ideas for the imaginary problem.**

Brainstormed ideas for the imaginary problem

- Dramatically increase the number of workers, e.g., 400 people at a time
- Use standard components
- Have a plan first
- Build components first
- Get legal/technical issues resolved
- Build on cement slab, not a full foundation
- Cut the size of the house in half
- Reduce the number of internal walls
- Use one color or no paint at all
- Walls that can be used inside and outside
- Modular bathrooms

- Hire subcontractors with specialties
- Have all materials on hand when needed but not in the way
- Have all participants in the process meet early
- Show up with coffee and donuts
- Have modular units contain subsystems (electrical, plumbing, etc.)
- Get financing up front
- Have 24 hour-a-day construction
- Quick hand-offs and simultaneous work schedules
- Build a house you can afford
- Have a piece of land first
- Have contracts with time clauses
- Get angry when schedules are missed
- Schedule time with no conflicts
- Do a PDPC (contingency plan)

7 **Apply ideas from the imaginary brainstorming back to the real problem statement.**

- In order to reconnect the imaginary brainstorming back to the real problem, it's helpful to ask:

    - Can one of the imaginary ideas be applied directly to the real problem as it's stated?

    - Can an imaginary idea be applied with some modification to the real problem?

    - Does the imaginary idea contain an original thought that could be the inspiration for a never-before-tried solution?

Sample Problem Application:

Imaginary Ideas	Apply	Application to the Real Problem
• Create modular components • Use standard components		• Design chapter templates with graphics built in *(Used with slight modification)*
• Do a PDPC (contingency plan)		• Do a PDPC to anticipate and resolve likely delays *(Used as is)*
• Cut the size of the house in half		• Simplify the content to cover only the essentials
• Have contract with time clauses • Get angry when schedules are missed		• Gain commitment to a firm schedule and stick to it *(Used as is)*
• Hire subcontractors with specialties • Have all materials on hand when needed but not in the way • Have all participants in the process meet early • Reduce the number of internal walls • Have 24 hour-a-day construction • Quick hand-offs and simultaneous work schedules		• Intensive authoring, editing, and layout process in which all of the participants and resources are in the same room at the same time. Off-site writing, editing, conferring, and desktop publishing are done

✔ If you need more breakthrough ideas, create a second imaginary problem statement and repeat Steps 5 through 7.

8. **Analyze all of the brainstormed ideas (real, imaginary, combined) and further explore the more interesting ones.**

   Consider any of the following tools:

   - Do an Affinity Diagram (see *The Memory Jogger™ II*, p. 12) to group all the ideas.
   - Do a Nominal Group Technique (see *The Memory Jogger™ II*, p. 91) to narrow down the number of ideas.
   - Do a simple Prioritization Matrix (see *The Memory Jogger™ II*, p. 105) based on key criteria to select the best ideas.

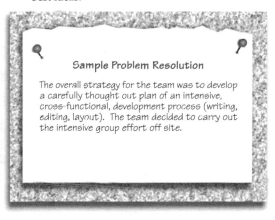

Sample Problem Resolution

The overall strategy for the team was to develop a carefully thought out plan of an intensive, cross-functional, development process (writing, editing, layout). The team decided to carry out the intensive group effort off site.

Case Example:
York Middle School

The Tale:

The York Middle School's budget was drastically reduced. As a result, a parent/teacher task force was formed to increase the number of parents who volunteer to help in the middle school.

The Team:

The team consisted of the middle school principal, two teachers, one parent who worked at home, and one parent who worked outside the home.

The Time:

A one-hour meeting.

The Task:

1. Define the goal or problem.

   Real Problem Statement: "How do we get more parents to volunteer to help at the middle school?"

2. Generate and record ideas using Classic Brainstorming.

Brainstormed ideas:

- Publish a list in the summer of volunteer work needed during the school year
- Get parents involved and excited about the curriculum
- Publish volunteer profiles in the newspaper
- Survey parents for their personal and professional skills
- For parents working outside of the home, schedule time in a single day
- Provide personal feedback to each volunteer
- Solicit help during the open house/orientation meeting
- Get the child and the parent to plan their work together
- Provide parents with a wide variety of potential volunteer activities
- Hold a telethon
- Create a buddy system among parents
- Hold an open house that brings together past volunteers and potential volunteers

3. Define the essential elements of the problem or goal statement.

Goal Statement: "How do we get more parents to volunteer to help at the middle school?"

The essential elements are:
- Parents (*Who is performing the action?*)
- To volunteer (*What is the action being performed?*) This is the essential outcome, don't change it!
- To help at the middle school (*What is the object of the action?*)

4. Propose imaginary replacements for one of the elements of the problem statement.

Essential Elements of the Problem	Possible Substitutions
Parents	• Soldiers • Orangutans • Politicians • Senior citizens • High school students • Martians
To volunteer	*Essential characteristic of the solution, don't substitute here!*
To help at the middle school	• To run a marathon • To learn a foreign language • To go into space on the space shuttle • To run for public office

5. Formulate a new problem statement, substituting one of the imaginary elements.

Imaginary Problem Statement

"How do we get more parents to volunteer to go into space on the space shuttle?"

6. Brainstorm ideas for the imaginary problem.

7. Apply ideas from the imaginary brainstorming back to the real problem statement.

Imaginary Ideas	Apply	Application to the Real Problem
• Have parents experience all phases of the flight through a simulator		• Have a volunteer fair that gives parents experience in the potential tasks needed
• Have astronauts meet personally with interested parents		• Have a famous parent personally meet with and lead potential volunteers
• Profile "ordinary citizens in space" on television		• Profile "volunteer parents" on local cable station, local newspaper, and internet home page
• Address the parents' fears		• Answer the parents' questions about the volunteer tasks
• Promise to talk to employers about needed time off for parents		• Work through the Chambers of Commerce to encourage employers to give parents time off to volunteer

Continued on next page

©1998 GOAL/QPC

• Describe in detail the training that parents will get	• Develop a volunteer Memory Jogger
• Develop a short public service video to be shown at movie theaters	• Create a "We Need You" public service video to be shown at the local movie theaters and cable television
• Tell parents that there will be a documentary made about them	• Profile "volunteer parents" on local cable station, local newspaper, and internet home page
• Recruit the kids to encourage their parents to apply	• Hold a contest for kid's classes that have the most parent volunteer hours

8. Analyze all of the brainstormed ideas (real, imaginary, combined) and further explore the more interesting ones.

The Tally:

The team was excited about ALL the new ideas they developed but decided to focus on these four activities specifically:

- Create a database of parent talents, hobbies, and professional skills
- Develop a "how to" Memory Jogger on the various volunteer tasks
- Get the most famous parent to do a public service video for local airing and lead the effort
- Develop a school-industry program to promote release time from work so parents can volunteer

Knowledge Mapping
Visual thinking

Why use it?

To graphically break down a broad goal or problem into increasing levels of detail to better understand the existing knowledge about it.

What does it do?

- Provides a team with a way to talk about, document, organize, and share its knowledge on a topic.
- Enables a team to build a picture of its current knowledge of a topic in order to identify gaps that must be filled so the team can reach its goal.
- Helps identify connections between key pieces of knowledge about an issue.

How do I do it?

1 **Assemble the right team.**
   - The team should consist of people who have up-to-date knowledge of, and a strong interest in the problem or goal statement.
   - The ideal group size is four to six people but a larger group may be accommodated as long as the ideas are visible and the session is well facilitated.

2. **State the goal or problem clearly.**
   - Typical sources of the problem statement:
     - An identified customer
     - The root cause or driver identified in an Interrelationship Digraph (see *The Memory Jogger*™ *II*, p. 76)
     - A refined problem statement from the Problem Reformulation tool

- The problem statement or "central theme" is usually written inside a black-edged cloud. This is the *"what"* that needs to be accomplished or understood more completely.

- The central theme is placed in the center of a flipchart or pinboard panel for further development of detail.

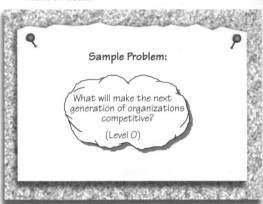

Sample Problem:

What will make the next generation of organizations competitive?

(Level 0)

3. **Generate the next lower level of detail, called "Initiatives" or Level 1 ideas, which are the major sub-goals to pursue.**

- Brainstorm "initiatives." These are the major "means" by which the problem statement can be achieved.

- An alternative approach is to do an Affinity Diagram on the problem statement. (See *The Memory Jogger*™ *II*, p. 12.) Brainstorm action statements and sort them into groupings, using the header cards as the initiatives.

Initiatives should be "functionally stated." A functional statement has three parts: an *action*, an *object*, and a *purpose* for the action. For example:

> **Incomplete Statement:**
> "Establish measurement systems."
>   **(action)   (object)**
> **(no statement of purpose)**
>
> **Complete Statement:**
> "Establish measurement systems."
>   **(action)   (object)**
>
> that improve processes and outcomes."
>   **(purpose of action)**

- *All* of the initiatives that are identified should be absolutely necessary to achieving the goal or solving the problem. The team should avoid including areas that are interesting but only loosely connected to the topic being discussed.

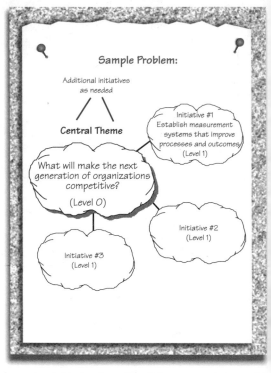

Sample Problem:

Additional initiatives
as needed

Central Theme

Initiative #1
Establish measurement
systems that improve
processes and outcomes
(Level 1)

What will make the next
generation of organizations
competitive?
(Level 0)

Initiative #2
(Level 1)

Initiative #3
(Level 1)

- An initiative is a *"how"* for accomplishing the "central theme" and becomes a *"what"* from a lower-level perspective.

✔️ To develop any of the initiatives into greater detail, post it on its own flipchart sheet or pinboard panel. To keep track of which topics and ideas go with that initiative, or to designate sequence, assign a numbering and/or lettering system, from the broadest level (the initiative), down to the most detailed level (supporting ideas.)

4. **Continue to generate the next levels of detail: Topics, Big Ideas, and Supporting Ideas.**

   • The simplest method for creating the lower levels of detail is brainstorming. A team should brainstorm ideas and then look to clarify, simplify, merge, or narrow them down to a few key areas.

   • Give each new level of detail its own color and/or shape to distinguish it from the other levels. This visual coding allows a team to more easily look for patterns and connections, as well as recognize the level in the hierarchy. Distinguishing each level by both shape and color is helpful, but not essential. Select at least one way (shape or color).

Level	Idea	Color/Shape	
0	Central Theme	Black/bold edged cloud	Central Theme (Level 0)
1	Initiatives	Red/thin edged cloud	Initiative (Level 1)
2	Topics	Green/ oval	Topic (Level 2)
3	Big Ideas	Orange/ circle	Big Idea (Level 3)
4	Supporting Ideas	Yellow/ rectangle	Supporting Idea (Level 4)

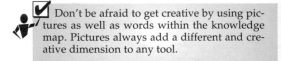

Feel free to change the names of the ideas at each level. Any name can be used as long as a legend is provided on the knowledge map that identifies the meaning of each symbol.

- Each level of detail is the "*how*" for accomplishing the level above it. Likewise, each level is the "*what*" for the level below it.
- Each shape is connected to its higher level with a line.
- When multiple ideas branch off of an idea, unless sequencing is vital, the ideas do not need to be in any specific order.
- All ideas, at least to Level 3 "Big Ideas," should be stated as functional statements. (See Step 3.)
- Develop as many levels of ideas as needed. The lowest level of detail will incorporate actions.

Don't be afraid to get creative by using pictures as well as words within the knowledge map. Pictures always add a different and creative dimension to any tool.

At any point in the knowledge mapping process, a team can add tools that would be helpful in further exploring an idea or task generated by the team. Techniques such as the Basic Quality Control Tools and/or the Management & Planning Tools can allow a team to make further progress once the map is finished.

©1998 GOAL/QPC

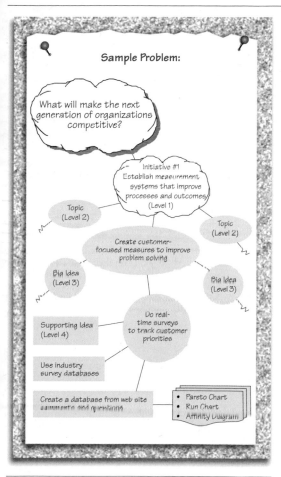

Sample Problem:

What will make the next generation of organizations competitive?

Initiative #1
Establish measurement systems that improve processes and outcomes
(Level 1)

Topic
(Level 2)

Topic
(Level 2)

Create customer-focused measures to improve problem solving

Big Idea
(Level 3)

Big Idea
(Level 3)

Do real-time surveys to track customer priorities

Supporting Idea
(Level 4)

Use industry survey databases

Create a database from web site comments and questions

- Pareto Chart
- Run Chart
- Affinity Diagram

5. **Interpret the knowledge map and determine next steps.**

- Examine the map, discuss it, and reorganize the ideas so that the team can answer these questions:
  - What does the team think and know about the problem in total?
  - Which ideas need to be further explored?
  - Can we connect some of the ideas in interesting, new ways?
  - Are there a few ideas that keep appearing in different places?
  - Are there other people in the organization that could help the team fill some of its gaps in knowledge about the problem?
- Continue to gather information through research, e.g., the internet, benchmarking, talking with others, and modify the map as appropriate.
- Identify the necessary action steps that must be accomplished to achieve the goal or solve the problem. Assign these steps to the appropriate people in the organization who can carry them out. Make sure to share the team's knowledge and ideas with the people who need it to explore key areas and/or carry out the work.

Variations

Mind Mapping is a widely known and practiced creativity technique first developed by Tony Buzan more than 20 years ago. It was first developed as a tool to help people to show graphically what the brain does naturally. The structure of the brain and the resulting thought patterns are both "tree-like." People take in, process, and remember information by connecting new ideas to an existing idea or group of ideas. These are the "branches" that help us make sense of the world and make new and creative connections.

Mind Mapping is very much like Knowledge Mapping in that it allows a team or individual to generate an enormous number of ideas by branching each idea into many more detailed ideas. The ideas in each branch can be either loosely or tightly connected with the "limb" from which it grew. To create a mind map, follow these simple steps:

1. **Write the topic (or draw a picture that represents it) in the center or extreme side of a sizeable piece of paper.**
   - Flipchart or butcher paper is great when working in teams. Ledger size (11" x 17") works well for individual work.

2. **Brainstorm ideas around the topic. For each major idea, draw a line directly from the main topic.**
   - Follow the guidelines for Classic Brainstorming.
   - Write the ideas directly on the lines.
   - The key ideas, such as the major branches, or clearly breakthrough ideas, should be printed most prominently (larger, all capitalized, a certain color, etc.).

3. **For each new idea, decide whether it is a new theme or a variation on an existing idea. Record ideas on the lines as they are generated.**
   - For new themes, draw a line directly to the main topic.
   - For variations on a previous idea, draw a line to that idea.

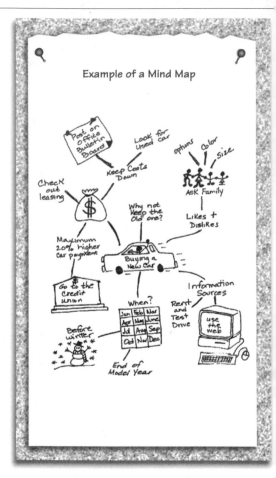

Example of a Mind Map

©1998 GOAL/QPC

4. **Continue thinking, drawing, and recording until the ideas (or the people involved) are exhausted.**

Knowledge Mapping and Mind Mapping Compared

Knowledge Mapping	Mind Mapping
• Uses standard shapes and/or colors to distinguish between ideas at different levels of detail.	• Ideas are recorded on lines with only major ideas visually set apart. There are no standard visual "markers."
• Ideas are expressed as functional statements that include a verb, object, and purpose of the action.	• Any idea, expressed in any way, is appropriate.
• Most effective when used by a team.	• Equally effective for use by an individual or a team.

Case Example:
Fostering Team Creativity

The Tale:

Century Insurance was losing business to several new competitors. These companies were introducing innovative changes more quickly than Century. The executive team formed a representative team to develop ways for teams throughout the company to become more creative in their work. After an initial two-hour meeting, the Executive Planning Team divided into sub-teams to further explore the major initiatives. One of these teams was a problem solving task force.

The Time:

A two-hour meeting.

The Task:

1. Assemble the right team.

A problem solving sub-team included the Vice President of Human Resources, a regional manager, an office manager, and a sales representative. The example shows the work of that sub-team.

2. State the goal or problem clearly.

3. Generate the next lower level of detail, called "Initiatives" or Level 1 ideas, which are the major sub-goals to pursue.

4. Continue to generate the next levels of detail: Topics, Big Ideas, and Supporting Ideas.

A. Align effort with corporate and customer priorities to avoid trivial pursuits

B. Pick the right team to get rich input of ideas

How can we foster team creativity so that better solutions can be developed?

C. Integrate the creativity tools into a problem-solving model to enhance quality and effectiveness of solutions

The team decided to focus on Initiative C. See next graphic for detail.

E. Create environment to support innovative team-centered problem solving

D. Train on appropriate skills to enable team members to work effectively

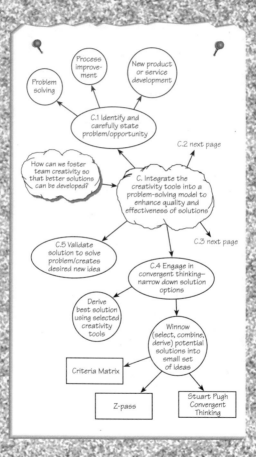

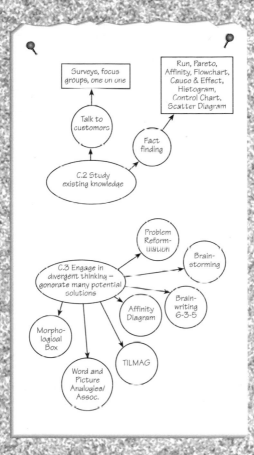

Surveys, focus groups, one on one

Run, Pareto, Affinity, Flowchart, Cause & Effect, Histogram, Control Chart, Scatter Diagram

Talk to customers

Fact finding

C.2 Study existing knowledge

Problem Reformulation

Brainstorming

C.3 Engage in divergent thinking – generate many potential solutions

Brainwriting 6-3-5

Affinity Diagram

Morphological Box

TILMAG

Word and Picture Analogies/Assoc.

5. Interpret the map and determine next steps.

The Tally:

The problem solving task force decided to pursue a three-part strategy in order to build the knowledge and skills of the entire company. It recommended that, at the very least, all managers should receive practical training in the Basic Quality Control Tools and the Creativity Tools so that they could help teams to:

- Identify and clarify problems and critical processes. Teams would therefore be more likely to be working on the most critical improvement areas.

- Open up their thinking patterns (practice "divergent thinking").

- Narrow down the best solutions from among the many creative options generated (practice "convergent thinking").

Morphological Box
*Anatomy of
a solution*

Why use it?

To map out all the combinations of potential solutions that address the essential parts of a problem.

What does it do?

- Helps to identify all of the parts of the problem that must be addressed to reach a successful solution.
- Builds a table that helps to display options for solving each essential part of the problem.
- Builds a table that helps a team to evaluate several solutions at one time.

How do I do it?

1. **Assemble a knowledgeable team.**

   - Unlike some of the other tools, the Morphological Box requires experts in the content area that is being discussed. These experts can join the team as needed or become permanent members.

2. **Define the parameters that are necessary for any solution to the problem.**

   - A parameter is a characteristic that a solution must possess in order for it to be effective.
   - A good parameter must:

     – Be independent from the other parameters.

     – Describe a complete solution when combined with the other parameters.

- Be valid for all potential solutions.
- Represent an essential characteristic of an effective solution.

Sample Problem:

"How can I determine which college is best suited for me?"

Problem Parameters
- Geographic location
- Student population
- Affiliation
- Specialization
- Total yearly cost
- Degrees offered
- Extracurricular options

There is no absolute rule for the number of parameters. However, when starting out, work from a list of six parameters or fewer. In general, five to ten parameters usually work well.

If you have difficulty identifying the parameters, do an Affinity Diagram (see *The Memory Jogger™ II*, p. 12) for the problem. Use the headers developed in the Affinity Diagram as the parameters.

- Create a table and place the selected parameters in the left-hand column of the table. The table should be large enough to fit all of the selected parameters and at least six cells to fill in the options for each parameter. (All six cells do not have to be used.)

Sample Problem:

"How can I determine which college is best suited for me?"

Parameters	Options							
Geographic Location								
Student Population								
Affiliation								
Specialization								
Total Yearly Cost								
Degrees Offered								
Extracurricular Options								

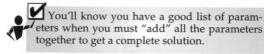

You'll know you have a good list of parameters when you must "add" all the parameters together to get a complete solution.

3. Generate options for each parameter.

- An option is an alternative within a parameter.
- Brainstorm a minimum of two options for each parameter. Each option must be independent from the other options.

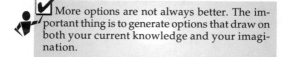

More options are not always better. The important thing is to generate options that draw on both your current knowledge and your imagination.

You'll know you have a good list of options when you usually would choose one "or" another of the parameters.

Sample Problem:

"How can I determine which college is best suited for me?"

Parameters	Options				
	Northeast	Mid-Atlantic	Southeast	Midwest	West
Geographic Location					
Student Population	<1000	1000-2000	2000-5000	5000-10,000	10,000+
Affiliation	Public	Private			
Specialization	Liberal Arts	Technical	Military		
Total Yearly Cost	Under $10,000	$10-20,000	$20,000+		
Degrees Offered	2 year only	4 year only	4 year + graduate		
Extracurricular Options	Sports/ Social	Intellectual/ Arts			

4. **Build alternative solutions by linking different options.**

- Within each parameter (row), select at least one option. The team can make this selection randomly (to maximize creative combinations) or systematically (to intentionally focus on specific combinations).

- Clearly mark the selected option(s) within the first parameter and draw a line to the selected option(s) in the next parameter. Continue to repeat this process until all selected options are connected by a line.

> Usually a single option is selected within a parameter. Select more than one option only when it will lead to more interesting combinations. Don't choose more options just to avoid making a choice.

- Develop alternative combinations of options by repeating the "mark and connect" process. Distinguish between the combinations of options by using differently marked points (e.g., boxes, triangles, circles) and connecting lines (e.g., solid, dotted, dashed). Be creative but also be clear.

Sample Problem:

"How can I determine which college is best suited for me?"

Parameters	Options				
Geographic Location	Northeast	Mid-Atlantic	Southeast	Midwest	West
Student Population	<1000	1000-2200	2000-5000	5000-10,000	10,000+
Affiliation	Public	Private	Technical		
Specialization	Liberal Arts	Technical	Military		
Total Yearly Cost	Under $10,000	$10-20,000	$20,000+		
Degrees Offered	2 year only	4 year only	4 year – graduate		
Extracurricular Options	Sports/ Social	Intellectual/ Arts			

Alternative #1 ☆   Alternative #2 ◯

5. **Analyze the alternative solutions and select the best one(s).**

- Even a modest sized Morphological Box can generate a large number of different combinations. In the sample problem, the Morphological Box can help a college applicant generate 2700 possible combinations of college profiles to consider.

> The number of combinations is determined by multiplying the number of options in the first parameter by the number of options in the second parameter, by the number in the third parameter, and so on to the last parameter. In the sample problem this would be 5 options in Geographic Location times 5 options in Student Population times 2 options in Affiliation . . . times 2 options in Extracurricular Options.
>
> Or, 5 x 5 x 2 x 3 x 3 x 3 x 2 = 2700!

- Clearly, the sheer number of possible combinations that a Morphological Box can create points to the need for a team to narrow down the number of combinations for evaluation. Possible evaluation methods include:

  –Intuitive: A team selects those combinations of options that it feels are the most promising or interesting. This works best with six parameters or fewer.

  –Optimization: The team selects the "best" option within each parameter and then combines these options to produce the one "best" combination across all parameters. However, the resulting combination may not actually work. The team would then have to substitute some options with the next best options in order to create a viable solution.

–*Sequential:* This method is essentially the same as the optimization method except that the team first considers the two, three, or four most important parameters and their options. For each of the remaining parameters, the team selects the options that look like the best combination with the options chosen for the most important parameters.

Sample Problem Resolution:

Chris, a high school junior enrolled in his school's military ROTC program, decided to consider Alternative #1 (the ☆ path).

In this combination, Chris thought the best-suited college would be in the **Mid-Atlantic** region of the United States, have a student population of **2000-5000**, would be a **public** institution with a **military** specialization, would cost less than **$10,000 a year**, and would be a **four-year** institution with an **intellectual/arts** extracurricular focus

Chris found that the U.S. Naval Academy in Annapolis, Maryland satisfied this combination. He quickly contacted his U.S. Senator for further details on the appointment process.

Case Example:

Designing a New Process for Selecting Managers at Compass Products

The Tale:

Compass Products, a small electronics assembly company, was poised for rapid growth. However, managers were leaving at an alarming rate. The management team concluded that the company had been hiring the wrong kind of managers. They set out to redesign the selection process.

The Time:

The team completed the Morphological Box during two 90-minute meetings.

The Task:

1. Assemble a knowledgeable team.

The redesign team consisted of the president, the operations and human resource managers, and two production supervisors.

2. Define the parameters that are necessary for any solution to the problem.

Parameters

- Participants
- Atmosphere
- Areas of inquiry
- Decision-making method for selecting the person
- Number of people interacting
- Process documentation
- Location of the process

©1998 GOAL/QPC

3. Generate options for each parameter.
4. Build alternative solutions by linking different options.

Alternative #1 ☆
Alternative #2 ○

Parameters	Options				
Participants	Peers	Reports	Bosses	Internal customers	Supplier
Atmosphere	Formal	Informal	Decision-making style	Communications style	Teamwork style
Areas of Inquiry	Technical knowledge	Values	Decision-making style	Boss's choice	
Decision Making Method for Selecting the Person	Consensus	Unanimity	Majority rules		
Number of People Interacting	One on one	Team	Audio		
Process Documentation	Notes	Video	Assessment center		
Location of the Process	Facility	Corporate office			

5. Analyze the alternative solutions and select the best one(s).

The Tally:

The Morphological Box made it possible (theoretically) for the team to consider as many as 3600 unique models for selecting a new manager. Out of the handful that it reviewed closely, the team chose two pilot models.

In the first pilot (), **a team** of **internal customers** would assess each candidate's **technical knowledge** by working with him/her in a **formal atmosphere** to solve a real operational problem at the **facility**. After the team reviews the **videotape** of the sessions, a candidate would be recommended based on the **consensus** of the team.

The second pilot () would include all of the candidate's **peers** holding **informal, one-on-one meetings** with the candidates at the **facility** in order to assess each candidate's fit with the core **values** of the organization. Based on each person's **notes**, the chosen candidate must be recommended **unanimously**.

©1998 GOAL/QPC

Picture Associations
and Biotechniques
Looking for inspiration

Why use it?

To move a team that is trapped in traditional thinking by using pictures and examples from nature as a way to stimulate fresh perspectives and new solutions.

What does it do?

- By describing in detail a picture or living thing from nature, unusual connections can be made to the problem.
- Provides an uplifting source of inspiration for breakthrough thinking.
- Creates a new focus point for the team's thinking that is very tangible, not philosophical.
- Re-energizes a brainstorming process that has reached a lull.

How do I do it?

1. **Define the problem clearly and brainstorm initial ideas.**

   - As always, the success of any creative thinking lies in the clear understanding of the problem. Take the time to ensure that everyone on the team is thinking and talking about the same issue in the same way.

   - Use Classic Brainstorming or Brainwriting 6-3-5 to surface the most obvious ideas for addressing the problem.

2. Determine which technique to use.

- Determine whether the team and/or the issue under discussion would benefit most from the use of Picture Associations or Biotechniques.

Picture Associations	Biotechniques
Use when:	**Use when:**
• Many of the team members are visual learners	• Nature does it better than humans do . . . borrow from nature to design a new and better product
• The team needs a real energy boost	• A team needs to understand the function of living things in mechanical terms
• You want to get people thinking in a number of dimensions	
• You want to appeal to multiple senses, intuition, or emotions	
Examples:	**Examples:**
To design a new chair, use random pictures like . . .	To design a reclining chair, study . . .
• A baby in an incubator	• The structure of a kneeling elephant
• Two people on a beach watching a sunset	• The anatomy of an elephant's flexing trunk

Continued on next page

Picture Associations	Biotechniques
Use pictures or models that:	**Use pictures or models that:**
• Are visually clear	• Show the structure of the animal in great detail
• Are positive, even inspirational	• Are anatomically correct
• Provide a fairly simple message	• Can be viewed from different angles
• Include more than one person or object	
• Are significantly different from the issue under discussion	
• Include a significant amount of activity, such as a major event or milestone	
• Create many different reactions and connections	

3. **Brainstorm associations or analogies that are stimulated by the selected picture or living thing.**

  • Definitions:

   An association: A mental connection that is triggered by an idea, a memory, a picture, or an event.

   An analogy: A comparison of a primary characteristic, action, or behavior between two things.

  • Choose a picture or representation of a living thing.

 Sources include magazines, books on nature, travel, encyclopedias, newspapers, photographs, the internet, compact disk libraries, and 3-D models.

  • Brainstorm ideas that come to mind when team members see the selected picture or living thing. As an aid to brainstorming ideas for a picture, consider the questions on the next page.

For Picture Association ask:

- What is going on in the picture?

- Who is doing what? How? Where? When? Why?

- What does the overall picture mean?

- What images does it call forth?

- What connections or comparisons can be made?

- What effects does the activity in the picture have on people? Nature?

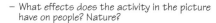

For Biotechniques ask:

– How does
   the living
   thing
   function?

– How does it
   breath?
   Perform
   other daily
   functions?

– What special
   problems does it solve?

– What special or unique features does the thing
   possess? How does it use these functions?

Once the team has chosen an interesting picture or model from nature, the team might conduct research (e.g., books, *National Geographic* magazine, the internet) to gain more knowledge about the functioning of that living thing. If the situation warrants, consider bringing in an expert.

• Record the ideas on the left side of a flipchart.

Sample Problem:

"How can we reduce the number of accidents in the plant?"

Type of technique: **Picture**
Picture: **Marching band**

Associations/ Analogies	Idea Related to the Problem
Everyone has to be in step	
A lot of instruments	
People in line	
Has a conductor/leader	
Enjoyable	
Music is loud enough to hear	
Every band has its own style	
Marchers love an audience	
Marchers wear a uniform	

4. **Take the ideas identified in Step 3 and restate them as they apply to the problem.**

   • In order to connect the brainstormed ideas for the picture/natural object back to the problem, it is helpful to ask:

     – Can one of the ideas be applied directly to the real problem as it is stated?

     – Can an idea be applied with some modification to the real problem?

     – Does the idea contain a truly original thought that could be the inspiration for a never-before-tried solution?

   • Examine an idea for an attribute, feature, or underlying concept that can be applied back to the real problem.

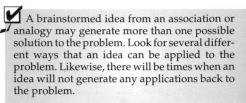

A brainstormed idea from an association or analogy may generate more than one possible solution to the problem. Look for several different ways that an idea can be applied to the problem. Likewise, there will be times when an idea will not generate any applications back to the problem.

Sample Problem:

"How can we reduce the number of accidents in the plant?"

Type of technique: **Picture**
Picture: **Marching band**

Associations/ Analogies	Apply	Idea Related to the Problem
Everyone has to be in step		• Safety rules must be consistently applied
A lot of instruments		• Customize safety guidelines for each piece of equipment
People in line		• People must be accountable to following the safety rules
Has a conductor/leader		• Must have someone to champion the safety effort
Enjoyable		• Contains an element of fun
Music is loud enough to hear		• Program reaches everyone • Program is so visible that people can't ignore it
Every band has its own style		• (Doesn't seem to apply to the issue? Keep thinking on this one!)
Marchers love an audience		• Recognize excellent performance
Marchers wear a uniform		• Have good standards in place • Give promotional t-shirts

5. **Repeat the process as often as is helpful, using a new picture each time. Pool the best ideas.**

- Generate more ideas by selecting another random picture and brainstorming ideas around that picture. (Repeat Steps 3 and 4 for each new picture.)

- Analyze the ideas and select the best ones for further study or next action steps. A team might:

  - Identify those ideas that are simple to accomplish and develop plans to implement them.

    - Use selection tools to identify the best ideas. Consider using any of these tools:

      a) Nominal Group Technique (see *The Memory Jogger™ II*, p. 91)

      b) Prioritization Matrices (see *The Memory Jogger™ II*, p. 105)

      c) Affinity Diagram to group the ideas, (see *The Memory Jogger™ II*, p. 12) and Interrelationship Digraph to prioritize the ideas (*The Memory Jogger™ II*, p. 76)

Case Example:
A New Design for a Child's Car Seat

The Tale:

A children's toy manufacturer, Fun-Time Toys, wants to enter the highly competitive child's car seat market. In order to succeed, the company must come up with a breakthrough design for a car seat that is innovative and safe.

The Time:

A 90-minute meeting.

The Team:

The Director of Product Development, a reliability engineer, a marketing representative, a sales person, and a botanist.

The Task:

1. **Define the problem clearly and brainstorm initial ideas.**

   Problem: "How can we design an innovative, safe car seat for a child?"

   - Make it lightweight to improve portability
   - Modular pieces that can be changed as the child grows
   - Color coordinated with car
   - Converts to a stroller
   - Seat turns to make it easier to get the child in and out of the car
   - and 15 more brainstormed ideas...

2. Determine which technique to use.

Type of technique: **Biotechniques**

Picture: **Cactus**

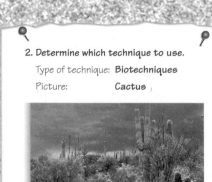

3. Brainstorm associations or analogies that are stimulated by the selected picture or living thing.

4. Take the ideas identified in Step 3 and restate them as they apply to the problem.

Associations/ Analogies	Apply > Idea Related to the Problem
Draws/stores water	• Water or gel filled seat pads for body warmth and extra comfort • Removable water supply: hot to keep warm, cold for cooling
Has a hollow core	• Double wall seat construction for strength, hollow core for light weight
Needles provide protection	• "Nubby" surface underneath provides non-slip surface
Colorful flowers attract birds for pollination	• Birds make homes in the cacti; have many small compartments or pockets to store kid's "stuff"

Associations/ Analogies	Apply	Idea Related to the Problem
Flowers come after rain, last for short period of time		• Toy entertainment center pulls out when needed, folds away when not needed • Use color body frames rather than just white or gray • Removable cloth covers available in a wide array of colors
Provides shade to small creatures		• Build in removable sun screen
Outer pulp expands like an accordion when water is absorbed		• Air bags that expand out from the safety seat to keep debris away
Has a tap root with even shorter radial roots		• An anchoring system that maintains its flexibility in a collision

5. Repeat the process as often as is helpful, using a new picture each time. Pool the best ideas.

The Tally:

The team developed a prototype for customer feedback that included the following features:

- Water or gel filled seat pads for body contour and extra comfort

- Removable cloth covers available in a wide array of colors

- Build in removable sun screen

- Air bags that expand out from the safety seat to keep debris away from the child

Problem Reformulation/ Heuristic Redefinition[1]

Envisioning a new approach to a problem

Why use it?

To help a team use pictures, questions, and criteria to take a fresh look at the components of a system in order to identify a fundamentally new approach to solving a problem.

What does it do?

- Turns a concept, product, or process and the system in which they exist into a picture. This ensures that everyone is looking at all of the components of the system and seeing them in the same way.
- Shifts a team's perspective so it can see a difficult problem as a system of connected parts.
- Uses the proven "who, what, where, when, why and how" questions to ensure that the team defines all of the components related to the problem.
- Prioritizes the components of a problem that lead the team to a restatement of the problem and to creative solutions.

How do I do it?

1. **State the problem or opportunity in terms of the improvement goal.**
   - Limit the statement to one sentence.
   - State the problem in broad, positive terms.

---

[1] Helmut Schlicksupp created this tool.

Limiting Problem Statement

"How do we stop children from making noise while they are waiting for treatment?"

- Possible solutions: discipline, restraints, give them candy

Better Problem Statement

"How do we help children wait patiently for treatment?"

- More positive and broader, i.e., does not focus on eliminating negative behavior

- Energizing

- Encourages creativity, e.g., keeping children comfortable and free of pain, allowing children to stay with their families

---

2. **Visualize the problem as part of a system.**

- Sketch a simple picture of the system in which the problem occurs. Use pictures, maps, stick figures, symbols, or icons. (See example on p. 5.)

Don't be afraid to draw, no matter what your level of artistic ability is. What's important is that all of the necessary components are clearly identifiable in the picture.

- Make sure all the components of the problem have been identified and drawn.

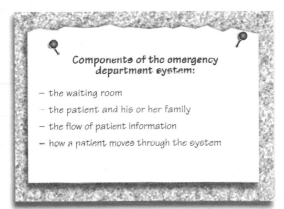

Components of the emergency department system:

- the waiting room
- the patient and his or her family
- the flow of patient information
- how a patient moves through the system

Having trouble defining the components of the system? Ask the "who, what, where, when, why, and how" of the problem.

In the emergency department example:

What is happening?

People are waiting, children are crying, staff are running. *Draw it!*

Where does it happen?

Parking lot, waiting room, examination room. *Draw it!*

When does it happen?

Shift changes, holidays, mornings or nights or weekends. *Draw it!*

How does it happen?

Children left alone, doctors or nurses are scary, wait is too long. *Draw it!*

Why does it happen?

Children remember past bad experiences, they're in pain, they're bored without toys. *Draw it!*

To whom does it happen?

Kids of different ages, a particular age group. *Draw it!*

Or who causes it to happen?

Doctors, nurses, parents, kids. *Draw it!*

- Based on the picture created by the team, list potential components and/or relationships and their definitions.

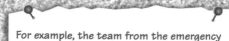

For example, the team from the emergency department listed these draft components:

- *information flow:* how information is communicated among staff and patients

- *staff interaction:* skills and attitude of staff when dealing with patients

- *waiting and treatment room environment:* the atmosphere and physical arrangements of rooms

- *arrival/welcome:* ease in check-in and welcome feeling for the patient and family

- *family connection:* can the family stay together?

- *staffing patterns:* mix of staff on duty at any time

- *patient mix:* adults, teenagers, senior citizens

3. **Discuss the ways in which each component affects the system. Label each component and/or relationship with a number.**
   - Understand the problem and the components of the system by addressing such issues as:
   a) What effect does each component have, either positively or negatively, on the problem statement? Confirm that each potential component has a significant effect. (Example shown on facing page.)

a) For example, regarding "patient mix," the team asks: "Are children more likely to wait patiently if they are . . .

- with kids their own age rather than adults, teenagers, senior citizens?"

- with people with similar injuries rather than people with different severities of injuries?"

"Patient mix" has an important effect on the goal and should clearly be one of the components of the system.

Review all of the other possible components in the same way to make sure each one is significant.

b) What are the influences or relationships between the components? Include both individual components and relationships. (Example shown on next page.)

c) Are there any scientific or natural laws that might affect the components in the system? (Example shown on next page.)

b) Emergency department example:

Individual components of the system

- information flow
- staff interaction
- waiting and treatment room environment

Relationships between components of the system

- Family connection = information flow + staff interaction + waiting and treatment room environment

c) In the emergency department example . . .

the time it takes for a medication to take effect may have to be considered when the emergency department team is defining the meaning of a "reasonable" waiting period.

- A team's discussion of the components may surface possible changes or additions. For example, a team may discover that a component is too broad or too similar to another component, and will need to revise the drawing.

Use the table below to help you determine whether a component is too broad, narrow, or unnecessary.

Examine Each Component

Too broad?	• large parts of a system	• break down to smaller components
Too narrow?	• finite • trivial	• combine • eliminate
Too similar to another component?	• little difference • no difference	• combine • eliminate one

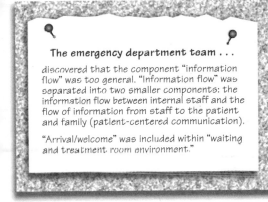

The emergency department team . . .

discovered that the component "information flow" was too general. "Information flow" was separated into two smaller components: the information flow between internal staff and the flow of information from staff to the patient and family (patient-centered communication).

"Arrival/welcome" was included within "waiting and treatment room environment."

- Number each of the components or the relationships between components.

In the emergency department example:

1. Internal information flow between staff
2. Patient-centered communication
3. Staff interaction
4. Waiting and treatment room environment
5. Family connection
6. Staffing patterns
7. Patient mix

4. **State the link between each component and the goal.**
   - Use each component or relationship identified in Step 3 to form questions that all start with: "How do we ensure that . . .?"

Component	"How do we ensure that . . ."
1. Internal information flow between staff	there is timely and accurate information exchange among all the appropriate staff members?
2. Patient-centered communication	there is timely two-way flow of information between staff and patient/family members?
3. Staff interaction	every staff interaction with the patient reflects both competence and concern?
4. Waiting and treatment room environment	the waiting and treatment rooms feel familiar and safe?
5. Family connection	the children are always close to the people they most trust?
6. Staffing patterns	there are always enough of the right kinds of people on staff?
7. Patient mix	children are waiting with other patients who have similar needs?

5. **Use a matrix to rate each component problem statement against team-selected criteria.**
   - Typical criteria might be:
     - Likelihood of reaching the goal
     - Ease of implementation of a potential solution
     - Expected impact on the overall goal, if it is achieved
   - Rate each component or relationship against the selected criteria using a simple rating scale. (See example on next page.)

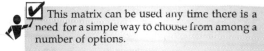 This matrix can be used any time there is a need for a simple way to choose from among a number of options.

6. **Discuss and choose the one or two problem statements that have the greatest potential for producing an innovative solution.**
   - The following items represent a typical selection process:
   a) Identify the item with the highest total rating in the prioritization matrix.

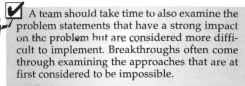 A team should take time to also examine the problem statements that have a strong impact on the problem but are considered more difficult to implement. Breakthroughs often come through examining the approaches that are at first considered to be impossible.

   b) Find out if there is consensus among team members that they are willing to tackle the selected problem statement. If there is no consensus, go to the next highest rated item and follow the tip above.

Problem Statement Prioritization Matrix

Rating:
3 = High/easy
2 = Medium
1 = Low/not easy

"How do we ensure that . . ."	Likelihood	Ease	Impact	Total
1. there is timely and accurate information exchange among all the appropriate staff members?	2	2	3	7
2. there is timely two-way flow of information between staff and patient/family members?	3	2	2	7
3. every staff interaction with the patient reflects both competence and concern?	1	1	3	5
4. the waiting and treatment rooms feel familiar and safe?	2	1	2	5
5. the children are always close to the people they most trust?	3	2	3	8
6. there are always enough of the right kinds of people on staff?	2	2	2	6
7. children are waiting with other patients who have similar needs?	2	2	1	5

c) As a next step, a team should use one of the other Creativity Tools to develop a list of potential solutions to the chosen problem statement.

In the emergency department example:

Component #5, "family connection" was the highest rated component with a total score of 8.

Potential creative solutions:

- A parent stays with the child before and during treatment in a private setting; the child trusts the parent and so feels safe and is more willing to wait patiently.

- A medical staff member is accessible to the family for questions and updates in order to maintain a flow of information.

- Make a television and age-appropriate books/magazines available in the rooms as an interesting way for the patient/family to pass the time.

- Have a computer in the room with Internet access.

Case Example:

Opening a Successful Airport Cookie Shop

The Tale:

SweetStuff ™ Cookies was a start-up operation that was going to be located in a just renovated terminal of a large regional airport. There was already a very successful cookie shop located near the point where passengers passed through airport security stations. The challenge was to develop a business concept that was disinctive, but that didn't interfere with *SweetStuff*™ Cookies' basic mission: **Sell cookies that people can't resist.**

The Team:

The team was made up of the two partners in the business and a friend from a marketing firm.

The Time:

The team completed the Problem Reformulation/ Heuristic Redefinition process during a 3-hour meeting at the home of one of the partners.

The Task:

1. State the problem or opportunity in terms of the improvement goal.

The team agreed that the problem/challenge was:

"How can we open and run a profitable, retail cookie shop at the Earhart Terminal?"

2. Visualize the problem as part of a system.

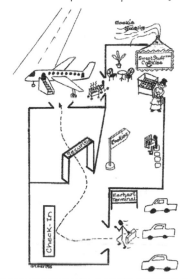

Components of the SweetStuff™ Cookies Store System	Definition
Store location	where the store is physically located in the airport terminal
Customer "attractors"	what physically draws people into the store
Cookie quality	the degree to which the cookies consistently meet or exceed customer expectations
Product pricing	the relative value of the product
Store atmosphere	the feeling that customers have when they're in the store
Product variety	the variety of product types and forms available to the customer
Product outlets	the different ways that cookies get into the hands (and mouths) of consumers

3. **Discuss the ways in which each component affects the system. Label each component and/or relationship with a number.**

The team reviewed each draft component for its clarity and relative impact on the goal statement. They felt that "product pricing" was actually a piece of "customer attractors," "cookie quality," and "product variety," and therefore could not be dealt with independently. All of the others stood on their own merits.

Sample Problem

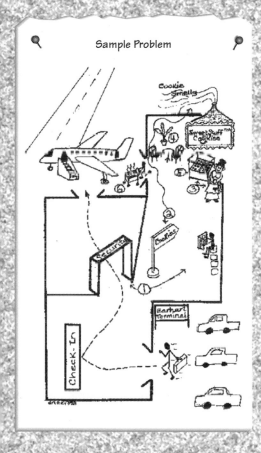

4. State the link between each component and the goal.

Component	"How do we ensure that..."
1. Store location	the store has the most convenient location in the terminal?
2. Customer "attractors"	people are drawn into the store in many ways?
3. Cookie quality	cookies consistently meet or exceed customer expectations?
4. Store atmosphere	customers feel welcome in the store and eager to return after they leave?
5. Product variety	all of the store's products are available in the form that customers want?
6. Product outlets	cookies get into the hands (and mouths) of consumers from a variety of outlets?

5. Use a matrix to rate each component problem statement against team-selected criteria.

Rating: 3 = High/easy
2 = Medium
1 = Low/not easy

Problem Statement Prioritization Matrix

"How do we ensure that . . ."	Likelihood	Ease	Impact	Total
1. the store has the most convenient location in the terminal?	1	1	3	5
2. people are drawn into the store in many ways?	3	3	3	9
3. the cookies consistently meet or exceed customer expectations?	3	2	2	7
4. customers feel welcome and eager to return after they leave?	2	2	2	6
5. all of the store's products are available in the form that customers want?	1	1	2	4
6. cookies get into the hands (and mouths) of consumers from a variety of outlets?	1	1	3	5

Problem Reformulation

6. Discuss and choose the one or two problem statements that have the greatest potential for producing an innovative solution.

The Tally:

Based on the prioritization matrix, the team decided that the most practical, effective path to take was to develop multiple ways to create "attractors." They decided to appeal to as many senses as possible...

Smell: ALWAYS have cookies baking in the oven, with aromas drifting into the terminal

Sight: an associate stands out front giving away "mini-cookies" as samples of daily specials

Sound: classical music can always be heard as people walk closer; SweetStuff™ Cookies is seen as a calm retreat from the craziness of travel

Good common sense: always offer great volume discounts

Some of the other problem statements, related to meeting and exceeding customer expectations and making customers feel welcome, were seen as absolutely necessary to long-term success (not a choice), but were not sufficient as means in such a crowded market to strongly distinguish SweetStuff™ from other cookie stores.

 **Purpose Hierarchy**
Thinking on purpose

Why use it?

To identify the full range of possible purposes of an improvement effort in order to choose the one that best fits the needs of the customer and the resources of the project team.

What does it do?

- Helps a team to identify a variety of purposes that it could choose to focus on.
- Allows a team to consciously decide on the size of the project that it intends to take on.
- Helps a team to use creative thinking to expand on an initial project purpose that may be overly narrow and modest.
- Helps a team to use practical analysis to narrow down an initial project purpose that may be ill defined and overly ambitious.

How do I do it?

1. **Assemble a team and state its purpose clearly.**

   - The team should consist of people who are familiar with and who have a clear interest in the problem under discussion. These people are often referred to as "stakeholders."
   - Write the initial understanding of the team's purpose on a flipchart or pinboard so that it is clearly visible to everyone on the team.
   - Any purpose statement should begin with the word "to" and have two parts: an *action* and an *object* of that action.

2. **Generate a range of possible purposes.**

- There are two ways for the team to generate a full range of purposes.

a) Progressive Questioning

- Start with the problem, as it is initially pre-sented, and ask: "What is the purpose of (<u>the problem purpose statement</u>)?" Apply this ques-tion to every successive answer.

> **For example:**
>
> Question 1: "What is the purpose of reducing the number of customer returns?"
>
> Answer 1: "To simplify product shipping and handling inside the company."
>
> Question 2: "What is the purpose of simplifying product shipping and handling inside the company?"
>
> Answer 2: "To reduce the cost of internal rework.
>
> Question 3: "What is the purpose of reducing the cost of internal rework?"
>
> Answer 3: "To improve customer satisfaction."

- Also try asking these questions when the team is looking for a full range of possible purposes:
  - What are we really trying to accomplish?
  - What are the purposes and needs of our customers?
  - What larger part of the system does this problem stem from?

> Common sense should be applied when deciding when the team has reached the broadest (and appropriate) purpose. The highest level purpose should be a "stretch" from the original yet still be closely connected to the original purpose statement.

b) Classic Brainstormed Method

- Write, legibly, one idea on a Post-it™ Note or card.
- Use an action verb and the object of the action.
  - Make sure that the verbs suggest a "total condition."
  - Do not use verbs that indicate increments of goals or objectives.
    Good Example:
    To improve service quality
    To improve student performance
    Poor Example:
    To reduce customer complaints by 25%
    To increase student test scores by 75 points

3. **Put a code on each Post-it™ Note or brainstormed idea to indicate the level of that possible purpose statement.**

   • Use a simple coding system to designate the possible levels into which any purpose statement could be placed. The codes do not necessarily mean "simple to do" or "complex to do." They refer to the scope or scale of the purposes relative to each other.

   Example:

   Simple purpose: "To fix the potholes on Main Street."

   Complex purpose: "To increase the efficiency of the transportation system in the city."

   The simplest way to test whether a purpose is "complex" is to ask, "Are there many ways to accomplish this purpose?" The more complex the purpose statement, the more optional ways there are to accomplish that purpose.

   • Typical coding:

"S"	for simple
"S-M"	for simple to medium
"M"	for medium
"M-C"	for medium to complex
"C"	for complex

   • Other levels of ordering might be:
     – Small to large
     – Immediate to long range

   It's not absolutely necessary to use Post-it™ Notes, but using them makes the sorting that's done in the following steps much easier. Post-its™ give the team the freedom to sort ideas as many times as is required to reach agreement.

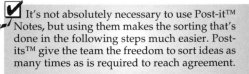

4. **Arrange all the possible purposes in the order of coding, from simple to complex, "S" to "C".**

- Place the possible purposes on a flipchart or a sheet of paper posted to a pinboard or wall.
- Place the lowest level of purpose (i.e., those marked with an "S") at the top of the sheet, working downward on the paper as the level progresses toward the more complex purposes.

 If several purposes appear to be at the same level, place the Post-it™ Notes side by side (if only temporarily). They can either remain at the same level or be re-sorted once the initial list is done.

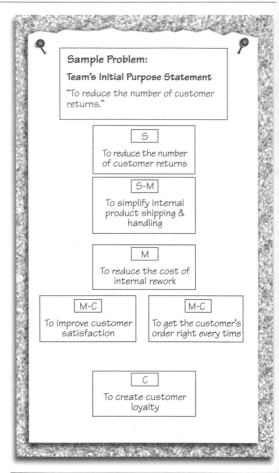

Sample Problem:

Team's Initial Purpose Statement

"To reduce the number of customer returns."

| S |
| To reduce the number of customer returns |

| S-M |
| To simplify internal product shipping & handling |

| M |
| To reduce the cost of internal rework |

| M-C |
| To improve customer satisfaction |

| M-C |
| To get the customer's order right every time |

| C |
| To create customer loyalty |

5. Analyze the "purpose list."

- The "purpose list" is the actual diagram of the grouped clusters of purposes.
- Look for gaps in the purpose array. Ask: "Are there any in-between levels that are left out?"

> ✔ If there is too big a gap between the purposes, management may agree only to the lower-level purposes on the list because they are perceived as less "risky."

- Check that the order is based on scope, not sequence. Rearrange the purposes on the list at any time you feel it's appropriate.

> ✔ Don't be afraid to expand the purpose list beyond what is possible to implement. What at first glance appears to be impossible may act as a bridge to more "practical" ideas.

6. Determine the criteria for selecting the "focus purpose."

- The "focus purpose" is the purpose selected by the team because it's viewed as being at the most effective level (scope or scale) compared to the other purposes.
- Possible criteria that can be used in selection of the focus purpose might be:
    - Potential benefits
    - Management's acceptance of it
    - Market or political environment
    - Resource needs
    - Time limitations
    - Organizational factors
    - Cost of the project

7. Select the focus purpose by applying the criteria.

- Not all criteria are equally important. The relative importance of each criterion is affected by:
  - an organization's financial situation
  - the priorities of key leaders
  - the actions of major competitors
  - the impact of current projects
- The simplest way to apply these criteria is to consider only the one or two factors that the team agrees are the most critical to the focus purpose.

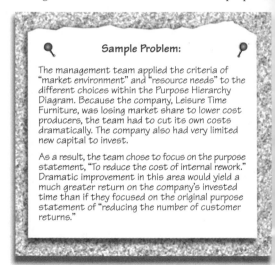

Sample Problem:

The management team applied the criteria of "market environment" and "resource needs" to the different choices within the Purpose Hierarchy Diagram. Because the company, Leisure Time Furniture, was losing market share to lower cost producers, the team had to cut its own costs dramatically. The company also had very limited new capital to invest.

As a result, the team chose to focus on the purpose statement, "To reduce the cost of internal rework." Dramatic improvement in this area would yield a much greater return on the company's invested time than if they focused on the original purpose statement of "reducing the number of customer returns."

Case Example:
Developing a "Global Business Language" Course Design

The Tale:

Based on the requests of many business leaders who were "going global," the curriculum committee of Twin Peaks Community College decided that a new kind of language course was needed. It had to meet the typical needs of people working alongside overseas colleagues and customers. Participants had to achieve their language goals in as short a time as possible.

The Time:

The committee met for two hours to agree upon their initial purpose.

The Task:

1. Assemble a team and state its purpose clearly.

The Team:

The heads of the language department and industry collaborative co-chaired a language curriculum sub-committee. The sub-committee also included a vice president of marketing, a veteran language instructor, a foreign national on temporary assignment with a local company, and a local manager who just returned from a one-year, overseas assignment.

Initial Purpose Statement:

To meet the typical language needs of people working alongside overseas colleagues and customers. Participants have to achieve their language goals in as short a time as possible.

2. Generate a range of possible purposes.

3. Put a code on each Post-it™ Note or brainstormed idea to indicate the level of that possible purpose statement.

The committee members decided to define the purpose of the new course based on the level of language skill that it would be designed to create for the student. They brainstormed and coded the following list of possible purposes.

- To be able to understand typical conversations in a foreign language. (M-C for "Medium to Complex")
- To be able to communicate basic daily needs in a foreign language. (S-M for "Simple to Medium")
- To be able to use a foreign language to understand the culture and history of that country. (M-C for "Medium to Complex")
- To be able to ask directions and order food in a foreign language. (S for "Simple")
- To be able to keep up an "average" social conversation in a foreign language. (M for "Medium")
- To be mistaken for a native of the country which language is being studied. (C for "Complex")
- To be able to go through an entire day without using the student's native language. (M-C for "Medium to Complex")

4. Arrange all the possible purposes in the order of coding, from simple to complex, "S" to "C".

To be able to ask directions and order food in a foreign language.
(S)

To be able to communicate basic daily needs in a foreign language.
(S-M)

To be able to keep up in an "average" social conversation in a foreign language
(M)

To be able to understand typical conversations in a foreign language.
(M-C)

To be able to use a foreign language to understand the culture and history of that country.
(M-C)

To be able to go through an entire day without using the student's native language.
(M-C)

To be mistaken for a native of the country which language is being studied.
(C)

©1998 GOAL/QPC

5. Analyze the "purpose list."

6. Determine the criteria for selecting the "focus purpose."

The sub-committee agreed that all the purposes were different from each other, but not to the point where any of them were radically different in scope or direction. They also decided that there were three key criteria to consider in selecting the best level purpose to address in the plan:

- Prepares students for both business and social situations.

- Can be done with students with no prior language training.

- Can be accomplished within a four to eight week period.

7. Select the focus purpose by applying the criteria.

The Tally:

The sub-committee decided to design the "Global Business Language" course aimed at producing students who would "completely understand typical conversations in a foreign language." Any lower level purpose would be easy to accomplish, but would prepare a student only to survive everyday life situations. Any higher level purpose would require three to four months of language immersion and exceed the skills needed to function during a one- to two-year overseas assignment.

TILMAG[1]
*Building ideal solutions
through associations
and analogies*

Why use it?

To systematically focus on those associations and analogies that will lead directly to a team's ideal solution.

What does it do?

- Forces a team to identify all of the necessary characteristics of an ideal solution.
- Provides an idea generation process that is more structured than the other tools and more tightly connected to a solution.
- Generates creative ideas based on paired combinations of the ideal solution elements.

How do I do it?

1. **State the problem clearly; brainstorm possible solution ideas.**

   - Use Classic Brainstorming or Brainwriting 6-3-5 to surface the most obvious ideas for addressing the problem.

2. **Identify and define Ideal Solution Elements (ISEs).**

   - TILMAG is a more guided thinking process than some of the other Creativity Tools. It uses the ideal solution as a starting point. The team identifies the Ideal Solution Elements (ISEs). An ISE is a function or attribute that any potential solution must have.

---

[1]TILMAG, created by Helmut Schlicksupp, is a German acronym that loosely translates as "the transformation of ideal solution elements in an association matrix."

- Create no more than six ISEs that are:
  - Specific for the given problem
  - Described in a positive way
  - Free of jargon
  - Brief (six words or less), but precise
  - Tied to customer demands (especially when developing a new product/service)

Sample Problem:

"To design the ideal Bed & Breakfast (B&B)."

Effective ISEs	Ineffective ISEs and Why
1. Feels like home	• Attractive (not specific to the problem) • Lacks the pizzazz of world class, state-of-the-art facilities (not positive; contains jargon; and too long)
2. Professionally managed	• No bugs (computer jargon; not specific to problem; not positive) • Well run (not specific to the given problem and not clear)
3. Priced to target market	• Affordable (less clear, open to different interpretations)
4. Variety of activities	• Not dull (not specific to the problem; not clear: could be interpreted to mean location, decorations, etc.; not positive)
5. Designed for a specific market	• Everyone loves it (not clear, not based on well-defined customer needs)

©1998 GOAL/QPC

3. **Construct an association matrix; write the ISEs on each axis (in top row and side column).**

- Write the ISEs on both axes.

  Option 1:

  - List all the ISEs sequentially, on both axes.
  - Block out or cross-out cells for each ISE paired against itself, or for duplicate pairings.

	1	2	3	4	5
1	X	X	X	X	X
2		X	X	X	X
3			X	X	X
4				X	X
5					X

or

	1	2	3	4	5
1	X				
2	X	X			
3	X	X	X		
4	X	X	X	X	
5	X	X	X	X	X

  - The size of the association matrix will vary according to the number of ISEs developed. In our example with five ISEs, a 6 x 6 cell matrix was set up. For four ISEs, set up a 5 x 5 cell matrix; for three ISEs, a 4 x 4 cell matrix; and so on.

  Option 2:

  - List the ISEs sequentially across the top, (except for the last ISE). List the ISEs down the side in reverse order, (except for the first ISE).
  - Block out or cross-out cells for each ISE paired against itself, or for duplicate pairings.

	1	2	3	4
5				
4				X
3			X	X
2		X	X	X

- This produces a smaller matrix with fewer blocked out cells. In this option, if there are four ISEs, create a 4 x 4 matrix, if six ISEs, create a 6 x 6 matrix.

4. **Brainstorm and record associations for each paired ISE.**

- For each cell, identify 2–3 associations (whatever comes to mind) between the paired combinations of any two ISEs.

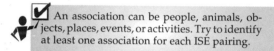 An association can be people, animals, objects, places, events, or activities. Try to identify at least one association for each ISE pairing.

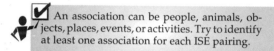 To preserve a spontaneous atmosphere in the team, don't be afraid to randomly go from cell to cell when creating associations.

- If an entire row or column is blank, perhaps that ISE is not as applicable as the team first thought. Either leave it as part of the matrix for future consideration or substitute another potential ISE.
- Continue the process until all the cells in the matrix have been addressed or the team has run out of time or energy. If needed, take a break before moving on to the next step.

Sample Problem:

"To design the ideal Bed & Breakfast (B&B)."

Association Matrix

	1. Feels like home	2. Professionally managed	3. Priced to target market	4. Variety of activities
5. Designed for a specific market	• Tupperware party • Antique or country furniture • Local convenience store	• Tailgate party • Wedding reception	• Mail order book club	• Senior citizen centers • Water park
4. Variety of activities	• Summer camp • Estuary	• Country club	• Game arcade • Ocean cruise	
3. Priced to target market	• Flea market • Bookstore cafes	• (Still thinking on this one . . .)		
2. Professionally managed	• Minor league baseball team • School open house • Church or synagogue			

5. **Transfer the underlying principle of each association back to the problem for possible solutions.**

   - List on a flipchart each association and the underlying principle(s) that came to mind when the association was made.
   - Next connect each association and its underlying principle back to the team's problem. This is where practical and imaginative thinking must come together.

Sample Problem:
"To design the ideal Bed & Breakfast (B&B)."
Association: Estuary

Principle or Feature	Connection to the Problem
• Many types of wildlife living together	• Have both common and private space, e.g., private bathrooms
• It is a safe haven	• Design facility within a nature/park setting
• A place to which species return each year	• A database of customer preferences that will help create a safe haven to which they will return
• Is a place to which species can retreat to when privacy is needed	• Provide profiles of fellow guests' interests and professions
	• Specialize in hosting reunions

Continued on next page

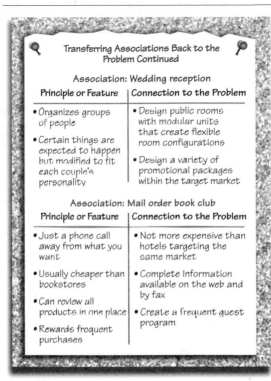

Transferring Associations Back to the Problem Continued

Association: Wedding reception

Principle or Feature	Connection to the Problem
• Organizes groups of people • Certain things are expected to happen but modified to fit each couple's personality	• Design public rooms with modular units that create flexible room configurations • Design a variety of promotional packages within the target market

Association: Mail order book club

Principle or Feature	Connection to the Problem
• Just a phone call away from what you want • Usually cheaper than bookstores • Can review all products in one place • Rewards frequent purchases	• Not more expensive than hotels targeting the same market • Complete information available on the web and by fax • Create a frequent guest program

6. **Pool the best ideas from both the TILMAG associa-tions and the initial brainstorming session.**

Case Example:

Reducing/Preventing Falls in Elderly Persons

The Tale:

A community's Office for Elder Affairs has been asked to address the problem of the increasing number of falls by the elderly. The office has been asked to institute a cost-effective, community-wide program that will reduce/prevent falls of elderly persons.

The Team:

Representatives from the Office of Elder Affairs, a geriatrics specialist, managers from a home care and nursing home organization, and two elder representatives (one male, one female).

The Time:

A luncheon and afternoon work session (no more than three hours).

The Task:

1. State the problem clearly; brainstorm possible solution ideas.

Problem: To institute a cost-effective, community-wide program that will reduce/prevent falls of elderly persons.

Brainstormed ideas

- Design sidewalks with elderly in mind
- Provide transportation
- Improve elderly services
- Teach elderly how to fall
- Keep elderly more fit
- Educate elderly in drug interactions
- Communicate learnings through public service announcements
- Review current data on falls to find root causes
- Educate the elderly on the dangers of falling
- Well designed retirement communities
- Improve aids for the elderly
- Design safer homes and buildings

2. Identify and define Ideal Solution Elements (ISEs).

Ideal Solution Elements

- Doesn't change lifestyle

- Easy to communicate

- Requires no costly equipment

- Builds self-esteem

- Effective both inside and outside the home

3. Identify and define Ideal Solutions Elements (ISEs).

4. Brainstorm and record associations for each paired ISE.

See Association Matrix on next page.

Association Matrix

	1. Doesn't change lifestyle	2. Easy to communicate	3. Requires no costly equipment	4. Builds self-esteem
5. Effective both inside and outside the home	• Gardening • Progressive dinners • Tai Chi	• Newspaper • Portable radio • Advertising jingle • Dance-step floor footprints	• Reading the newspaper/book • Playing cards • Bird watching	• Pets • Storytelling • Making things yourself
4. Builds self-esteem	• Courses on television • Joining a club • Singing in a chorus	• Praising people • Teaching	• Breaking a bad habit • Walking • Crossword puzzles	
3. Requires no costly equipment	• Listening to favorite radio station			
2. Easy to communicate				

5. Transfer the underlying principle of each association back to the problem for possible solutions.

Association	Principle or Feature	Connection to the Problem
Gardening	• Caring for things that grow • Seeing results of your efforts • Very hands-on oriented	• Teach them to monitor and chart their calcium intake • Monitor their muscle and bone strength
Portable radio/ listening to favorite radio station	• Provides information/ entertainment • Connects you with the world • Moves with you	• Develop public service announcements for the elderly by the elderly who have increased their strength levels • Develop a wearable monitor that senses imbalance and sounds a warning
Walking	• Healthy • Gets you outdoors	• Develop special elderly nature/ walking trails with periodic stops for resting and/or simple exercises

Continued on next page

Transferring Associations Back to the Problem Continued

Association	Principle or Feature	Connection to the Problem
Teaching	• Sharing your knowledge • Pride in other's accomplishments	• Set up networking opportunities for the elderly to share health advice, experiences recovering from falls, prevention tips
Joining a club	• Opportunity to interact with others • Find or be with friends • Pursue an interest	• Develop an "Adopt an Elder" Program to take the elderly on walks outside the home (nature, shopping, sightseeing). The walk could help them increase their strength

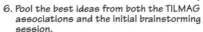

6. Pool the best ideas from both the TILMAG associations and the initial brainstorming session.

The Tally:

Develop a team (including a geriatric specialist, a physical therapist, a nutritionist, a psychologist, and a trainer) whose purpose is to put all of the tools for preventing/reducing falls into the hands of the elderly.

The team's main strategy is to develop a comprehensive mind and body program that would be implemented at each of the four senior citizen centers in the community. The program would include a combination of the ideas that were generated in the TILMAG process and the Classic Brainstorming session, while meeting the conditions that were set forth by the ISEs.

Word Associations and Analogies

Making connections and comparisons

Why use it?

To move a team that is trapped in traditional thinking by using random, unrelated words as a way to stimulate fresh perspectives and new solutions.

What does it do?

- By describing a random word, object, or situation in detail, unusual connections can be made to the problem.
- Provides a virtually unlimited supply of inspiration for breakthrough thinking.
- Enables all team members to create a new focus point for their thinking.
- Re-energizes a brainstorming process that has reached a lull.

How do I do it?

1. **Define the problem clearly and brainstorm initial ideas.**

   - As always, the success of any creative thinking lies in the clear understanding of the problem. Take the time to ensure that everyone on the team is thinking and talking about the same issue in the same way.
   - Use Classic Brainstorming or Brainwriting 6-3-5 to surface the most obvious ideas for addressing the problem.

2. Determine the source of stimulating words to use.

- Determine whether the issue under discussion is a technical or non-technical problem.

Technical or Object-Related Problems	Non-Technical or Process/Strategy-Related Problems
Examples:	**Examples:**
• Designing a new chair	• Entering a new market
• Correcting a product failure	• Planning a conference
• Developing a better voice mail system	• Creating a community volunteer organization
• Redesigning a company brochure	• Improving the hiring process
Word Sources:	**Word Sources:**
• Random Word List for Technical Problems (page 159)	• Random Word List for Non-Technical Problems (page 160)
• Also consider a thesaurus, dictionary, newspaper, magazine, or book	• Also consider a thesaurus, dictionary, newspaper, magazine, or book

✓ These are meant to be helpful guidelines, but the flexibility of this technique lies in its randomness. Don't be afraid to use a word from any source to create innovative connections and solutions.

3. **Brainstorm associations or analogies that are stimulated by the selected picture or living thing.**

- Definitions:

  An association: A mental connection that is triggered by an idea, a memory, a picture, or an event.

  An analogy: A comparison of a primary characteristic, action, or behavior between two things.

  Light as air

  Swims like a fish

  Gentle as a whisper

- Choose a word from the technical or non-technical word list or other selected sources. If using the word lists on pages 159 and 160:

  Have a team member call out a random number between 1 and 60, or the current "seconds" reading on a watch. Using that number, select the matching random word from the list.

  – Close your eyes and point to somewhere on the list, and select the word under your finger.

  If using other sources:

  – Have a team member call out a random page number, then a position on that page, and select the nearest word or object.

- Brainstorm ideas that come to mind when team members think of the selected word.

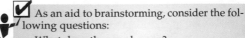

As an aid to brainstorming, consider the following questions:

– What does the word mean?
– What images does it call forth?
– What connections or comparisons can be made?
– How is the object structured?
– How does it function?
– How is the object used?
– What effects does it have on people? Nature?

• Record the ideas on the left side of a flipchart.

Sample Problem:

"How do we encourage people to take responsibility for their own training needs?"

Type of problem: **Non-technical**

Time on watch: **10:49 AM**

#49 random word: **Roller coaster ride**

Associations/ Analogies	Idea Related to the Problem
Stomach churning	
Wind in face	
Weightless	
Hands up	
Adventure	

4. **Take the ideas identified in Step 3 and restate them as they apply to the problem.**

- In order to connect the brainstormed ideas for the random word back to the problem, it's helpful to ask:
  - Can one of the ideas be applied directly to the real problem as it is stated?
  - Can an idea be applied with some modification to the real problem?
  - Does the idea contain a truly original thought that could be the inspiration for a never-before-tried solution?
- Examine an idea for an attribute, feature, or underlying concept that can be applied back to the problem.

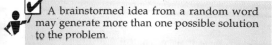

A brainstormed idea from a random word may generate more than one possible solution to the problem.

Sample Problem:

"How do we encourage people to take responsibility for their own training needs?"

Type of problem: **Non-technical**

Time on watch: 10:**49** AM

#49 random word: **Roller coaster ride**

Associations/ Analogies	Apply	Idea Related to the Problem
Stomach churning		• Job security is dependent on getting training
Wind in face		• Put training announcements in company newsletter
Weightless		• Make it easy for people to register (self-register) • Provide a computer program that allows people to read, select, and register themselves for the training • Take the burden of registration off of staff
Hands up		• Volunteer for training
Adventure		• Encourage innovative training • Encourage people to take training out of town

5. Repeat the process as often as is helpful, using a new word each time. Pool the best ideas.

- Generate more ideas by selecting another random word and brainstorming ideas around that word. (Repeat Steps 3 and 4 for each new word.)

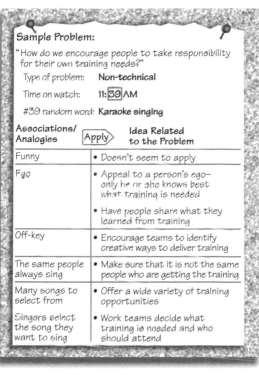

Sample Problem:

"How do we encourage people to take responsibility for their own training needs?"

Type of problem: **Non-technical**

Time on watch: 11:**39** AM

#39 random word: **Karaoke singing**

Associations/ Analogies	Apply	Idea Related to the Problem
Funny		• Doesn't seem to apply
Ego		• Appeal to a person's ego—only he or she knows best what training is needed
		• Have people share what they learned from training
Off-key		• Encourage teams to identify creative ways to deliver training
The same people always sing		• Make sure that it is not the same people who are getting the training
Many songs to select from		• Offer a wide variety of training opportunities
Singers select the song they want to sing		• Work teams decide what training is needed and who should attend

- Analyze the ideas and select the best ones for further study or next action steps. A team might:
  - Identify those ideas that are simple to accomplish and develop plans to implement them.
  - Use selection tools to identify the best ideas. Consider using any of these tools:
    a) Nominal Group Technique (see *The Memory Jogger*™ *II*, p. 91)
    b) Prioritization Matrices (see *The Memory Jogger*™ *II*, p. 105)
    c) Affinity Diagram, to group the ideas, (see *The Memory Jogger*™ *II*, p. 12) and the Interrelationship Digraph, to prioritize the ideas, (*The Memory Jogger*™ *II*, p. 76)

Case Example:
Office Space Reduction

The Tale:

Two companies have merged their headquarter operations, which are now located in one of the company's facilities with dramatically less floor space for offices.

The Team:

A joint team across the two companies, including two facility planners, a Management Information Systems administrator, and the manager of Human Resources.

The Time:

A 45-minute planning meeting.

The Task:

1. **Define the problem clearly and brainstorm initial ideas.**

   Problem: "How to assist staff in adjusting to limited office space?"

   - Provide a break room for staff
   - Use smaller pieces of furniture in the offices
   - Allow staff to work at home part of the time
   - Make sure the offices have windows
   - Encourage people to share a space with friends
   - Bring in a specialist in office organization
   - Share equipment that is used only occasionally

Continued on next page

- Allow people to choose the color of their own office space
- Put in sound deadening materials or equipment
- Schedule more meetings to minimize the amount of time spent in their offices
- Start an affirmative action program fo r small people
- Schedule more frequent breaks
- Make sure that all of the offices are the same size
- Have monthly "clean your office" days
- Hang large scale art pieces above the cubicles
- Require that all books purchased be no larger than a Memory Jogger!

2. **Determine the source of stimulating words to use.**

   The team chose to use the random word list for non-technical problems. (See p. 160.)

3. **Brainstorm associations or analogies that are stimulated by the selected word.**

4. **Take the ideas identified in Step 3 and restate them as they apply to the problem.**

Problem: "How to assist staff in adjusting to limited office space."

Type of problem: **Non-technical**

Time on watch: **3:12 PM**

#12 random word: **State fairs**

Associations/ Analogies	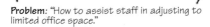 Apply > Idea Related to the Problem
Smells	• Improve environment
Cotton candy	• Snack area
	• Very comfortable meeting space
Pat Boone	• Pipe in live music or radio
Temporary tents/rides	• Set up modular offices with no fixed walls
Tent raising	• Have everyone participate in the set up of the office and have a follow-up party
Games	• Allow games on computers
Horses	• Free and convenient parking
Competitions	• Compete for the most efficient use of space

Continued on next page

Associations/ Analogies	Apply ▷	Idea Related to the Problem
Fun	• Create common spaces that are stimulating
Merry-go-round	• Allow people to decorate their own "space"
Contest	• Doesn't seem to apply
School holiday	• Office party and end-of-fiscal-year celebration
Sheep shearing	• Get rid of junk in offices

5. **Repeat the process as often as is helpful, using a new picture each time. Pool the best ideas.**

The Tally:

The team chose a few key strategies for the transition to less office space:

• Develop a very comfortable and private common area for people to meet.

• Hold a contest for designing the most efficient use of space.

• Have everyone participate in the design and set up of the office space and have an "office raising" party.

To randomly choose a word, have a team member look at a watch and call out the number that he or she sees in the digital display or sweep of the second hand. Find and use the word associated with that number.

Random Word List for Technical Problems

This list includes objects; no actions or events.

1. toothbrush	16. light bulb	31. eye	46. watch
2. wine	17. rabbit	32. dragon	47. unicorn
3. elephant	18. soap	33. cheese	48. tailor
4. baseball bat	19. violin	34. bayonet	49. silver
5. bird	20. diamond	35. moose	50. sombrero
6. book	21. clothes hanger	36. motorcycle	51. river
7. cup	22. butter	37. pickle	52. pretzel
8. pipe	23. monk	38. hammer	53. orange
9. whale	24. rainbow	39. barrel	54. mirror
10. seashell	25. sand	40. garlic	55. letter
11. robe	26. steam	41. oasis	56. flea
12. window	27. leaf	42. mayonnaise	57. umbrella
13. fork	28. helicopter	43. bubble gum	58. dice
14. ball	29. giraffe	44. toga	59. ant
15. chair	30. fountain	45. frog	60. coffee

Random Word List for Non-Technical Problems
This list includes actions and events only; no objects.

1. presidential election	16. speeding	31. beauty contest	46. first day at school
2. olympic games	17. World Series	32. evening news	47. sending a valentine
3. high school graduation	18. poker game	33. baking cookies	48. Halloween
4. senior prom	19. April 15 (taxes due)	34. camping	49. roller coaster ride
5. spelling bee	20. aerobics	35. New Year's Eve	50. meeting future in-laws
6. getting a driver's license	21. Thanksgiving Day	36. losing weight	51. moving day
7. Watergate	22. Boston Marathon	37. wine tasting	52. eating lobster
8. wedding	23. bingo	38. jumping rope	53. first day of spring
9. tennis match	24. finger painting	39. karaoke singing	54. snow storms
10. boot camp	25. fishing	40. solar eclipse	55. high tide
11. family vacation	26. house painting	41. corporate retreat	56. end-of-season sales
12. state fairs	27. jury duty	42. conference call	57. garage sales
13. Earth Day	28. debates	43. car buying	58. spring cleaning
14. Fourth of July	29. Christmas	44. going to the zoo	59. wall papering
15. dental exam	30. barbecue	45. learning to swim	60. birthdays

Chapter **5**

Other Great Stuff

This chapter includes seven more ways of thinking. These techniques are a small sampling of how you can get your creative juices flowing to think in new ways and approach problem solving more effectively.

Use this chapter as a starting point, not a final destination: seek out as many creative techniques as you wish or have time to investigate. The more ways you look at something, the more open and flexible your mind will be.

Ask Child-like Questions

Do you remember as a child how many questions you asked? Why is the sky blue? Why do zebras have stripes? Why can't we fly? As an adult, you probably ask a lot fewer questions at the risk of appearing ignorant or childish. The creative adult, however, makes a conscious effort to question the status quo, to be suspicious of existing answers and approaches, and to ask "silly" questions.

For example, did you know that the concept of "instant photographs" was born because someone asked the right "silly" question? Edward Land was taking pictures of his family while on vacation in the Southwest. His young daughter asked, "Why do we have to wait to see the pictures?" Land thought to himself "Good question!" He sketched out some ideas and when he returned to his lab in Boston he tested them out. The Polaroid Camera and the science of instant photography were created soon thereafter.

Ask Why Five Times

When there's a problem, a person's natural response is to ask why the problem is occurring. Don't stop at asking why just one time though, ask why at least five times to be sure you get to the root of the problem.

1. **Why did an employee fall down in the hall?**
   The employee slipped on a puddle of water

2. **Why was there a puddle of water in the hall?**
   There is a leak in the skylight

3. **Why is there a leak in the skylight?**
   It was not installed properly

4. **Why wasn't the skylight installed properly?**
   Because the boss (and owner of the building) asked his brother the plumber to install it

5. **Why did the boss ask his brother to install it?**
   Because his brother said he would do it for free

Re-installation of the skylight by a qualified person will solve the problem. Why not ask why for your problem?

Ask Who? What? Where? When? Why? How?

It can be difficult to look at all the aspects of a problem at once. Instead, try focusing on one aspect at a time. The more specifically you define the parts of your problem, the easier it will be to generate ideas for a solution.

Who . . .

- might be involved in the problem?
- may have special strengths, resources, or access to useful information?
- might gain from a resolution of the problem?

What . . .

- are the requirements of the situation?
- are the difficulties or risks involved?
- are the pro's and con's of formulating a resolution?

©1998 GOAL/QPC

Where is the problem occurring?

- Consider location; place; focal points of the problem.

When is the problem occurring?

- Consider schedules; dates; timeliness of the situation.

Why is the problem occurring . . .

- at a certain place, location or sequence in the process?
- at a particular time of the day, week, month, year?
- with a certain person, group, or division?

How . . .

- are people or objects affected by the problem?
- is time or space affected by the problem?
- does the problem change if something in the environment is changed?

Change Your Assumptions

When you're driving, you assume that other drivers will also obey the traffic rules. When you purchase a stereo or computer, you assume that directions for setting it up will be included. However, if you're looking for a new perspective, angle, or twist on a problem, any assumptions you've made can be deadly to the creative process!

When you change your assumptions, you open the door to a new world of ideas. Use the steps below as a guide.

1. **List all your assumptions about your problem.**

2. **Change your assumptions, one by one.**

   - Ask what the opposite or reverse of your problem would be. If you want to increase the number of words you type a minute, think about decreasing this number. What would you have to do?

   - Change a positive statement into a negative statement. If you want to provide good customer service, list ways that you could make it bad.

- Try to define what something is **NOT**. Ask what everyone else is **NOT** doing.

- Make up a list of opposing actions that you can apply to the problem. What will happen if you: stretch it/shrink it?; freeze it/melt it?; personalize it/depersonalize it?

- Change your most basic assumption about something; pretend it doesn't exist. What is the new reality?
  - What if gravity stopped for a minute every day?
  - What if a house could only be one of three colors, based on the amount it's worth?

- Turn defeat into victory. If a situation turns sour in the end, come up with some positive aspects of the experience.

3. **Ask yourself how to accomplish each change of assumption.**

4. **Choose a solution and build it into a realistic idea.**

Construct an Idea Matrix

An Idea Matrix is a great tool for inventing a new product, new concept, new market, a new name for something, or alternative ideas for solving a problem. It allows people to ask themselves questions that they may not think to ask. A single Idea Matrix, or a series of them, can be used to generate ideas for almost any situation. For example:

- Landscape designers can use them to produce variations of gardens;

- Adventure companies can use them to combine ideas for activities and trip participants;

- Anyone can use them to generate ideas on how to combine their personal objectives and skills.

An Idea Matrix is a grid with a set of parameters across the top (x axis) and another set down the side (y axis). One parameter from the top is matched with a parameter from the side to generate ideas for that combination of parameters.

For example, an activities coordinator who works for an adventure company may start by thinking of the possible parameters for "trip participants" and "activities." (See example on next page.)

The coordinator would create the matrix and look at the combinations of parameters, marking the ones that looked particularly interesting and plausible.

Another example: Stan Mason, an inventor and new product consultant, asked himself if he could invent a more nutritious and less fattening, on-the-go breakfast treat than a cup of coffee and a doughnut. He set up a series of grids that included items like "Where" the snack might be available, and "When" it might be eaten. Then he thought up different parameters for each item, such as home, office, vending machine for "Where"; and breakfast, lunch, tea time, anytime for "When." Ultimately, Stan Mason's use of the Idea Matrix led to the invention of the granola bar![1]

Create a Storyboard

You can "storyboard" anything: the plot and characters of a mystery novel, the tasks and people needed to carry out a project, or the construction of your dream house. This can be done as you are doing it or as you think it should happen.

A storyboard shows, at any point in a process, project, or problem-solving situation, the flow of ideas, actions,

---

[1]Bryan W. Mattimore, *99% Inspiration: Tips, Tales & Techniques for Liberating Your Business Creativity* (New York: ANACOM, 1994, 95–97.

Possible Combinations of Activities and Trip Participants

Trip Participants	Back-packing	Skiing	Sailing	Kayaking	Whitewater Rafting	Scuba Diving
					Activities	
Singles			☆		☆	
Couples	☆		☆	☆		
Families	☆		☆	☆		
Children		☆	☆			
Teenagers	☆		☆		☆	
Senior Citizens						☆

tasks, objects, and people and how they are interconnected. With your ideas on a storyboard, you can see how one idea relates to another, and how all the pieces come together. You can move ideas around, insert new ideas, piggyback on other people's ideas, make new combinations, get rid of ideas, and "shape the storyboard" as much as you want, until you're happy with the story.

Walt Disney and his staff developed a storyboard system in 1928. Disney wanted to achieve full animation and for this he needed to produce an enormous number of drawings. Managing the thousands of drawings and the progress of a project was nearly impossible, so Disney had his artists pin up their drawings on the studio walls. This way, progress could be checked, and scenes added and discarded with ease.[2]

To create a storyboard, start with these basic materials: a corkboard or corkboard-like surface; index cards; push pins; markers or pens; and pictures (optional).

Write the topic on an index card and pin it onto the corkboard. Under the topic card, pin header cards that have general points/categories written on them. Under the header cards, pin sub-header cards, which have the detailed ideas that were generated in a brainstorming session. From here, you're ready to add, delete, and move around ideas as you think through (or live through) the tasks of a project, the plot of that mystery novel, or the process of getting your house built.

Look into TRIZ

With the increasing demands on the speed with which problem solving is done or with which new products move from customer need to concept to development to market, a technology that increases the speed of invention is needed. TRIZ is one way to meet that need.

---

[2]Charles Cave, web site www.ozemail.com.

TRIZ, which in Russian stands for "Theory of Inventive Problem Solving," is a set of methods and principles that helps people to examine problems and quickly develop many solutions. It is especially useful for new product development, service delivery, and solving production problems. It has helped people produce dramatic results:

- In two hours an automotive supplier came up with 60 patentable ideas for improving a component that had been inadequate for five years.

- In two days, a powder metallurgy problem that had persisted for 10 years was solved, eight different ways.

- A new design concept for a hydraulic hammer design that had a four-year history of field failure was developed in the first half-day of analysis.[3]

Genrich S. Altshuller and others devoted more than 50 years of research into understanding how inventive or breakthrough solutions were found. This research defined 11 conceptual elements that have been used to solve problems and produce patentable solutions.

The 11 elements of TRIZ are grouped into two categories, Problem-Solving Tools and Analysis Models. The "Tools" category includes: 40 Principles, S-field Analysis and Standards, and ARIZ (Algorithm for Inventive Problem Solving. The Analysis Models category includes: Ideality, Contradictions, Levels of Innovation, Evolution of Technical Systems, Functional Value Analysis, Consolidation, Trimming Techniques, and Failure Prevention.

The problem-solving methods are used to generate solutions (or solution concepts or potential solutions). The analysis models influence the solution concepts.

---

[3]GOAL/QPC Research Committee, *TRIZ: An Approach to Systematic Innovation* (GOAL/QPC, 1997), 5.

Chapter **6**

Activities to Enhance Creativity

Creativity is exciting and fun, however, some people see creativity as something mysterious, uncontrollable, and available to only a privileged few.

While we may not all be on the same creative playing field as Albert Einstein, Michelangelo, Wolfgang Amadeus Mozart, Pablo Picasso, or Julia Child, we do have the ability to be creative.

Creativity is about seeing things differently and coming up with fresh, new ideas.

What is it that enables some people to be more creative than others? Creative work comes out of mind-sets that are established within physical, mental, and emotional states. While it is different for everyone, creative people tend to:

- know the best time of day for working
- create a particular or unique environment to work within
- analyze and question the "facts" and common beliefs
- work hard and keep at it
- enjoy what they are doing
- let the mind wander or intensely focus their thinking
- think creatively as much as possible: they practice, practice, practice

To build on this last point of practicing creativity, there are a variety of activities that can be used to "loosen up" a team's or individual's thought patterns. Use them to encourage a creative "mood" or as a way to prepare to use any of the Creativity Tools. (See Appendix A for solutions to Activities 2 and 6.)

Activity 1: Things Are Shaping Up

Creative thinking is often about taking old ideas and/or new ideas and seeing them or combining them in different ways.

For example, two very common shapes—a triangle and a rectangle—can be combined to produce two different things: a house or a rocket. How can you combine the triangle and rectangle into something different?

Now try using the shapes below to see how many ideas you can create by combining them. Or make up your own two or three shapes and combine them into something new.

Activity 2: Hidden Meanings

GESG   Everyone loves a "play on words." For starters: these letters are "scrambled." When you unscramble them you get the word "eggs." Put them together and you get "scrambled eggs!"

Now try to figure out what the words and shapes in the boxes on the next page stand for. (See Appendix A for the solutions.)

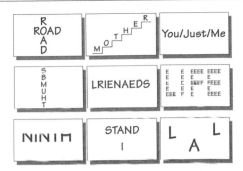

Were these too easy? Have your team members create their own "hidden meaning" puzzles and challenge each other.

Activity 3: On a Cloudy Day

Once upon a time we would lie in a field, look at the sky, and see things in the clouds . . . dragons, sailing ships, elephants . . . the possibilities seemed endless.

Maybe we all can't watch passing clouds, but we can draw a simple free-form shape, study it, and then turn it into a creative picture. Examples:

Each person should now quickly sketch a free-form shape and let his or her imagination and pencil run wild!

Activity 4: Common Things . . . Uncommon Uses

Many creative ideas have come from thinking of new uses for existing things or ideas. For example, children around the world are using backpacks to carry their worldly possessions to and from school. Backpacks were only for hikers and soldiers until fairly recently. One way to stretch our thinking is to choose any common object and describe its uses in its normal setting. Now choose a very different setting and list all of the different ways it could be used. Example:

A baseball bat . . . is used in a *baseball game* to:
- hit the ball
- clean baseball spikes
- stretch muscles

could be used in a *rain forest* to:
- hunt for food
- scare away predators
- hold up a lean-to
- rescue someone from quicksand
- ?

Choose your own objects and settings and go exploring.

Activity 5: Word Scramble

Think of a word (8 letters or more) or a short phrase from within your discipline or area of expertise. Try to make as many 3-, 4-, 5-, or more letter words from the word or phrase as you can.

For example, if you work in a hospital setting, you might think of "operating room." From this you could create opera, germ, moot, more, poor, grate, grape, etc.

Some words and phrases to get you started:
- Imagination
- Morphological Box

- Story telling
- Problem Reformulation

What's your record number of words?

Activity 6: Finding the Missing Link

We've all had conversations in which someone makes a comment that leaves everyone wondering, "Where did that come from?" Maybe that person really wasn't listening. Or maybe something that was said set off a string of connections that ultimately turned into that off-the-wall remark. The problem is that all of those interim connections were invisible to everyone else in the group.

For example:

Clean my office
↓
Need a bulldozer
↓
My yard sure needs some landscaping
↓
It's supposed to be hot this weekend
↓
There's nothing like ice-cold watermelon
↓
I have to stop at the fruit stand on the way home

Try to identify 3–4 "missing links" between the following statements:

- Are we ready for the trade show next week?
- ?
- ?
- ?
- ?
- Where is my high school yearbook anyway?

(For the solution, see Appendix A.)

Give the group a common question and ask them to write down their first five thoughts. Ask someone to volunteer his or her last thought and have fun "finding the missing links."

Activity 7: Adding Up Idea #1 + Idea #2 = Wow!!!

Some of the most ingenious inventions have come from taking old ideas and giving them a twist.

In 1951, Betty Nesmith combined white tempera, water-based paint (idea #1) and a small nail polish bottle (idea #2) to create Liquid Paper to paint over her typing mistakes![1]

In 1975, Ed Pauls, in preparing for an upcoming cross-country race, was faced with terrible outdoor weather. So he wondered about combining a cross-country workout (idea #1) with skiing indoors (idea #2) to come up with his indoor ski machine, Nordic Track![2]

In 1893, George Washington Gale Ferris Jr. combined the chair (idea #1) with a wheel (idea #2) to create the Ferris Wheel.[3]

See how many different ways you can combine the following things to create a new idea:

- water + plastic bag = ?
- ball + string = ?
- fire hydrant + lamp = ?

Now think up your own ideas and combine them in new ways.

---

[1] Allyn Freeman & Bob Golden, *Why Didn't I Think of That? Bizarre Origins of Ingenious Inventions We Couldn't Live Without* (New York: John Wiley & Sons, 1997), 36–40.

[2] Ibid, 65–69.

[3] Tom Wujec, *Five Star Mind: Games & Puzzles to Stimulate Your Creativity and Imagination* (New York: Doubleday, 1995), 115.

A: Answers to Activities

Activity 2: Hidden Meanings (p. 171)

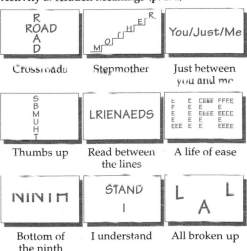

R ROAD A D	^H^E^R M^O^ᵗ	You/Just/Me
Crossroads	Stepmother	Just between you and me
S B M U H T	LRIENAEDS	E E CEEE FFEE FF EE E E E E EEEE EEEE EE E E E EEE E E EEEE
Thumbs up	Read between the lines	A life of ease
NINIH	STAND I	L L A
Bottom of the ninth	I understand	All broken up

Activity 6: Finding the Missing Link (p. 173)

- Are we ready for the trade show next week?
- *I've got to make arrangements to get to the trade show.*
- *I think I'll fly.*
- *I remember my first flight—a high school graduation present.*
- *I went with Randy, my best friend.*
- Where is my high school yearbook anyway?

B: References, Resource Groups, Web Sites

References

Adams, James L. *Conceptual Blockbusting: A Guide to Better Ideas.* Reading, MA: Addison-Wesley Publishing Company, Inc., 1986.

Altshuller, G. S. *And Suddenly the Inventor Appeared: TRIZ, the Theory of Inventive Problem Solving.* Worcester, MA: Technical Innovation Center, Inc., 1996.

Buzan, Tony with Barry Buzan. *The Mind Map Book: How to Use Radiant Thinking to Maximize Your Brain's Untapped Potential.* New York: PLUME by the Penguin Group, 1996.

Gardner, Howard. *Creating Minds: An Anatomy of Creativity Seen Through the Lives of Freud, Einstein, Picasso, Stravinsky, Eliot, Graham, and Gandhi.* New York: Basic Books, a Division of HarperCollins Publishers, 1993.

Kao, John. *Jamming: The Art and Discipline of Business Creativity.* New York: Harper Business, a Division of HarperCollins Publishers, 1996.

King, Robert and Helmut Schlicksupp. *The Idea Edge: Transforming Creative Thought into Organizational Excellence.* GOAL/QPC, 1998.

Michalko, Michael. *Cracking Creativity: The Secrets of Creative Genius.* Berkeley, CA: Ten Speed Press, 1998.

Nadler, Gerald and Shozo Hibino. *Breakthrough Thinking: Why We Must Change the Way We Solve Problems, and the Seven Principles to Achieve This.* Rocklin, CA: Prima Publishing & Communications, 1990.

Peters, Tom. *The Circle of Innovation: You Can't Shrink Your Way to Greatness.* New York: Alfred A. Knopf, 1997.

Plsek, Paul E. *Creativity, Innovation, and Quality.* Milwaukee, WI: ASQC Quality Press, 1997.

von Oech, Roger. *A Whack in the Side of the Head: How You Can Be More Creative.* New York: Warner Books, 1983.

This list is by no means exhaustive on the topic of creativity. Check the bibliography sections in each of these books for more ideas. Don't forget to read biographies of creative people such as Maya Angelou (poet, author), Marie Curie (scientist), Thomas Edison (inventor), Albert Einstein (scientist), Benjamin Franklin (inventor and statesman), Georgia O'Keefe (artist), Leonardo da Vinci (artist and inventor), and Lily Tomlin (actress, writer, comedian).

Resource Groups

Creative Education Foundation
1050 Union Road
Buffalo, NY 14224

Phone: 716-675-3181
Fax: 716-675-3209
E-mail: cefhq@cef-cpsi.org
Web site: http://www.cef-cpsi.org

National Center for Creativity Inc.
6845 Parkdale Place, Suite A
Indianapolis, IN 46254

Phone: 317-639-6224 or 1-800-306-6224
Fax: 317-387-3387
E-mail: NCCIINDY@aol.com
Web site: http://www.creativesparks.org

Web Sites

Use any of the internet search engines to search on the words "creativity" or "innovation." Try combining these words with other improvement techniques and tools, e.g., problem solving. Have fun following the links but beware: some are good, but many are not. Also, search often. Information on the internet changes all the time. What may be there today will be gone or different tomorrow.

Ordering Information: 5 Ways to Order

CALL
TOLL FREE
1-800-643-4316
or 603-893-1944
8:30 AM – 5:00 PM EST

MAIL
GOAL/QPC
2 Manor Parkway
Salem, NH
03079-2841

WEB SITE
www.goalqpc.com

FAX
603-870-9122

E-MAIL
service@goalqpc.com

Price Per Copy

1–9	$7.95
10–49	$6.95
50–99	$6.25
100–499	$5.75
500–1999	$5.50

For quantities of 2000 or more, call for a quote.

Sales Tax
Canada 7% of order

Shipping & Handling Charges
Continental US: Orders up to $10 = $2 (US Mail).
Orders $10 or more = $4 + 4% of order (guaranteed
Ground Delivery). Call for overnight, 2 & 3 day
delivery. **For Alaska, Hawaii, Canada, Puerto Rico
and other countries, please call.**

Payment Methods
We accept payment by check, money order, credit
card, or purchase order. **If you pay by purchase order**:
1) Provide the name and address of the person to be
billed, or 2) Send a copy of the P.O. when order is
payable by an agency of the federal government.

Order Form for
The Creativity Tools Memory Jogger™

1. Shipping Address (We cannot ship to a P.O. Box)

Name _____

Title _____

Company _____

Address _____

City _____

State _____ Zip _____ Country _____

Phone _____ Fax _____

E-mail _____

2. Quantity & Price

Code	Quantity	Unit Price	Total Price
1055E			
		Tax Canada only	
		Shipping & Handling See opposite page	
		Total	

3. Payment Method

❏ Check enclosed (payable to GOAL/QPC) $ _____

❏ VISA ❏ MasterCard ❏ Amex ❏ Diners Club ❏ Discover

   Card # _____ Exp. date _____

   Signature _____

❏ Purchase order # _____

Bill to _____

Address _____

City _____

State _____ Zip _____ Country _____

4. Request for Other Materials

❏ Information on products, courses & training

❏ Information on customization

Customization of Your GOAL/QPC Books

Customize GOAL/QPC products with your company's name and logo, mission or vision statement, and almost anything else.

Benefits of customization
- Allows you more flexibility in determining content
- Gives your leaders an opportunity to personalize every copy
- Helps to promote your company's quality improvement efforts
- Communicates your organization's commitment to quality
- Helps lower the costs of in-house development of training materials
- Helps employees understand how they can help achieve company goals
- Gives your team a common vision

A few details
- Please allow a minimum of *4 weeks* for delivery of customized products.
- Customization is most cost effective for quantities of *200 or more.*
- Ask us about customizing GOAL/QPC products in other languages.
- We're flexible on what and how much can be customized; almost anything is possible. Just call us and ask.

The Idea Edge: Transforming Creative Thought into Organizational Excellence

The Idea Edge is the perfect companion to *The Creativity Tools Memory Jogger™*. It is designed to provide your coaches and team leaders with helpful hints, examples, and application studies for creating breakthrough solutions. *The Idea Edge* describes step-by-step use of idea generation tools, and includes additional tools for selecting from the best ideas, and successfully implementing them to create breakthroughs for your organization.

Code: 1034P

The Memory Jogger™ II

This pocket guide is designed to help you improve the procedures, systems, quality, cost, and yields related to your job. *The Memory Jogger™ II* combines the basic Quality Tools and the Seven Management and Planning Tools in an easy-to-use format. It includes continuous improvement tools such as Cause and Effect, Histogram, Run Chart, Pareto Chart, and many more!

Code: 1030E

Quantity discounts are available.

The Team Memory Jogger™

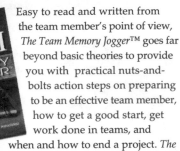

Easy to read and written from the team member's point of view, *The Team Memory Jogger*™ goes far beyond basic theories to provide you with practical nuts-and-bolts action steps on preparing to be an effective team member, how to get a good start, get work done in teams, and when and how to end a project. *The Team Memory Jogger*™ also teaches you how to deal with problems that can arise within a team. It's perfect for all employees at all levels. Available in Spanish.

Code: 1050E

The Memory Jogger™ 9000/2000

The Memory Jogger™ 9000/2000 will guide you through the latest modifications to the ISO 9001 standard, with easy-to-follow instructions to prepare for, implement, and maintain ISO registration. This powerful pocket guide provides each employee with a clear understanding of the changes in terminology and clause structure from the 1994 standard, and answers key questions about each employee's role in the registration process.

- Updated ISO 9001:2000 clause names and structures, paraphrased and organized into easy-to-follow sections. Comparison of ISO 9000:1994 and ISO 9001:2000 clause structures

- Examples, notes, pitfalls, and illustrations to foster understanding *Code: 1065E*

Problem Solving Memory Jogger™

The Problem Solving Memory Jogger™ is an easy-to-use pocket guide designed to help teams or individuals use a 7-step method to solve organizational problems. This method includes several data analysis and decision-support tools that enable teams and individuals to clearly describe process-related problems, isolate their root causes, create effective solutions, and standardize process improvements so the problem does not occur again.

Code: 1070E

Facilitation at a Glance!

This pocket guide, written by Ingrid Bens and co-published by GOAL/QPC and AQP, describes facilitation behaviors and tools, the stages of facilitation, best and worst facilitator practices, how to facilitate conflict during meetings, effective decision making, techniques for getting everyone to participate, and much more. The many examples, checklists, and surveys can help anyone master the skills needed to facilitate meetings effectively.

Code: 1062E

Quantity discounts are available.

Coach's Guide to The Memory Jogger™ II CD-ROM Package

The *Coach's Guide Package* makes it easier than ever to use *The Memory Jogger™ II* as a key resource in your effective training efforts. You can get your teams to better use the basic quality control tools and management and planning tools so that they can achieve their objectives and improve their self-sufficiency in solving problems.

The tools included are: Activity Network, Affinity, Brainstorming, Cause & Effect, Check Sheet, Control Chart, Flowchart, Force Field Analysis, Histogram, Interrelationship Digraph, Matrix, Nominal Group Technique, Pareto, Prioritization Matrices, Process Capability, Radar, Run, Scatter, and Tree.

Each tool has a set of overheads that includes these features: • a summary of the steps for using the tool • an overview of the steps in flowchart form • illustrations of the tool at different steps • finished examples of the tools

The CD-ROM Package includes:
- 1 *Coach's Guide*
- 1 CD-ROM disk with 187 overheads in Microsoft PowerPoint™
- 5 copies of *The Memory Jogger™ II*

You can print the overheads as you need them and you can customize them too!

Code: 1046

Quantity discounts are available.